CADET NO. 1

First published in India in 2021 by HarperCollins Children's Books
An imprint of HarperCollins *Publishers*
A-75, Sector 57, Noida, Uttar Pradesh 201301, India
www.harpercollins.co.in

2 4 6 8 10 9 7 5 3 1

Text and illustrations © Maya Chandrasekaran
and Meera Naidu

P-ISBN: 978-93-5422-855-1
E-ISBN: 978-93-5422-895-7

Typeset in 12.5/16 Amiri
by Tanvi Sahu

Printed and bound at
Thomson Press (India) Ltd.

This book is produced from independently certified FSC® paper
to ensure responsible forest management.

CADET NO. 1

AND OTHER AMAZING
WOMEN IN THE ARMED FORCES

MAYA CHANDRASEKARAN
& MEERA NAIDU

HarperCollins*Children's Books*

OFFICER 4971

WG. CDR. DR V RAMANAN (VSM)

OFFICER 4971 – WG. CDR. DR V RAMANAN (VSM)
The life and interesting times

This is the story of Officer 4971. Otherwise known as Wing Commander V Ramanan. Otherwise known as Dr Vijayalakshmi Ramanan. Otherwise known as the Officer with the nose rings. Otherwise known as the first woman in the Indian Air Force.

But before she was all that, she was TN Vijayalakshmi, or Vijaya, or Vijayam (meaning victory), which is what her family called her.

Vijaya (1924–1939)

Vijaya was born in 1924, bang in the middle of a family of seven siblings. Her father worked in the Postal Services, which reported to the ruling British Government at the time. It was a transferable job, and Vijaya and her family moved around every three or four years. She was used to starting from scratch in every new city and every new school, especially as she had her siblings (her gang) with her.

And everywhere they went, the house reverberated with music. Her family was part of the great tradition of Carnatic music, so wherever they were transferred, celebrated musicians visited them, both to teach the children and perform informally for the family.

In many ways, it was a charmed life, and despite the constant upheaval, the children were happy and close. At every posting, they found places in the local school and quickly settled in.

Growing up, Vijaya had many ambitions, mostly around performance

– to be a singer or a bharatnatyam dancer (although she never learnt dance formally). Maths and Science were her favourite subjects in school (winning her the nickname 'Brainiac' then and later in life), but if anyone asked her what her ambition was, she would never have said 'doctor'. At that time, she had no real role models, apart from

the members of her family. Growing up with so many siblings was tremendous fun, but also meant that she rarely had to look outside her world for inspiration.

But somewhere inside was an instinct for healing, and it became impossible to ignore. When they were posted in Trichy, the house had a large garden with plants of various kinds. Vijaya used to spend hours there, crushing leaves to make 'medicine' and hand it out (force it on them, she later remembered gleefully) to family members for their 'illnesses'. It gave her father and uncle a hint of what might lie in her future.

Vijaya's father, T.D. Narayana Iyer, was a war veteran and had fought for the British in World War I. He was proud of his work with the government, and he passed on this sense of service to the children. Without realizing it, they grew up understanding that they had a duty. That duty called out to them in different ways.

When she was fifteen, Vijaya had her first broadcast on All India Radio (AIR), along with her older sister, Kamakshi, from AIR Trichy. Kamakshi would go on to become a radio artiste. Vijaya had expected to be nervous – she had performed before many times, but always in homes and in front of family and friends. This time it was different – it was professional, in a studio, surrounded by strangers. When she entered the room, she looked around and got a sense of everything and everyone there, before sitting down quietly. Maybe it was her sister's presence, or just the familiarity of the music, but she felt instantly comfortable in front of the microphone. The accompanists started. As always, the music lifted her out of herself, and she performed without even thinking. When it was done, she felt a rush of exhilaration – a feeling she would later learn was adrenaline. She was now an official performer, and even got paid a (very small) cheque for her services. It was the first of a lifetime of professional musical performances and she was immensely proud of it.

That same year, it was also time for her to go to high school – it was called Intermediate in those days. Her family was posted in Tranquebar (on the coast of Tamil Nadu) at that time, but for Vijaya, life was going to change now. Rather than moving schools every two years, her parents decided it was time for her to settle down in one city and focus on getting her degree.

Viji (1939–1943)

Madras.

Today, after much chaos and uncertainty, I got admission to Intermediate in Presidency College. I always thought I would study in Madras at Queen Mary's College but last week my cousin sent us a telegram: no seats available at any Madras College for Vijaya. All seats taken (!!)

Appa and I panicked. I didn't want to lose a year! I couldn't lose a year after all that hard work!

We took the next train to Madras to visit all the colleges. But it was true. There was nothing in Queen Mary's College. We tried next at WCC but there they told me I'm underage. My last option was Presidency College – it's the only other one with women students. Again, all the seats were full. By this time I was losing hope.

But Uncle came to the rescue. He suggested that Appa take an appointment with the Principal of Presidency College – Prof. Harold Charles Papworth. I wasn't allowed to join him at that meeting, so I paced about at home.

It worked! I don't know which one did the trick – Appa's persuasive skills and his description of us as a family or the 25 rupee contribution to the Presidency College Alumni Fund. But it worked!

It was not my first choice. Queen Mary's is still my favourite college. But everyone says that Presidency is one of the best in Madras.

I think it will be fine.

I will stay at the Queen Mary's hostel with the other girl students and study Science at Presidency.

I think I'll be the only girl in the Science Section.

I wonder how that will be.

One day, while Vijaya and her father were in the stationery store buying college supplies, they bumped into a distant relative – Dr K.S Viswanathan and his son, Ram. At that point Vijaya was too shy to even look up and make eye contact. She focused on her books, as any proper Brainiac would, and honestly didn't think much of that encounter. Unexpectedly though, she and Ram kept in touch, and later they would decide to get married. But that was years later, after many other interesting things had happened *to* her and *around* her.

By the time she had completed her Intermediate, Vijaya had made up her mind that she was going to be a doctor. It was an unusual choice, but like her music, it just felt natural. She had realized that all of her games administering 'medicine' came from a desire to help and heal people. She now also had some powerful female inspirations—women she was reading about, hearing about and even meeting in pre-Independence Madras—Sarojini Naidu and Dr Muthulakshmi Reddy.

Winds of change
Prof. Harold Charles Papworth was the last in a line of British academics to serve as Principal of Presidency College. His successor in 1943 was Dr B.B. Dey, a sign of winds of change across India.

Sarojini Naidu

The Path-Breakers

Dr Muthulakshmi Reddy was a pioneering medical practitioner, social reformer and legislator. She was responsible for abolishing the Devadasi system in Tamil Nadu and was a close friend and colleague of Sarojini Naidu.

Sarojini Naidu was a poet, politician and one of the foremost freedom fighters in India. She was the first woman president of the Indian National Congress and the first woman governor of an Indian state.

Individually, they were inspirational. Together, they were incredible role models for what strong, talented women could achieve.

Vijaya applied to medical college but was rejected for being too young. It felt like another set-back, like not getting into her college of first choice. She felt like every time she moved forward one step, she was stalled. Disheartened, she was not sure what to do next, when Dr K.S. Viswanathan re-emerged in her life, with some helpful advice. There was nothing wrong, he said, with doing a graduate degree before medical college. Becoming a doctor was a big undertaking, and at her age, she wasn't ready for all that it meant.

Vijaya took his advice and enrolled for a B.Sc. at Presidency College, studying Chemistry, Botany and Zoology. She continued to stay in the Queen Mary's hostel. In retrospect, she was happy with her decision to be just another student for a little longer.

Her student days were filled with science, representing Presidency in intercollegiate competitions and music. With one of the older girls in the hostel acting as chaperone, the girls were allowed out to attend all the kutcheris (musical concerts) they could desire. By now, she was an established radio artist as well, singing on what was considered prime time on AIR (All-India Radio) regularly, and even receiving her own fan mail. It was a happy, carefree time.

The country was in the throes of the Quit India movement and the Freedom struggle. Where they were in South India, and in college, Vijaya felt largely untouched by the revolution. Her father's position as a government servant was a strong factor. As a veteran of WW1 and a British government servant, he was uncomfortable with the family showing obvious support for the movement. But it was impossible for anyone to be completely unaffected by the movement.

Living in a hostel with a British matron meant that the girls had to be discreet about their political feelings. But they were young and fired up by national passions, and sometimes they just couldn't hold themselves back.

One evening, when the girls were marching around the courtyard with their 'Quit India' banners and their slogans, the girl on lookout duty suddenly yelled, 'Watch out! Matron!' In seconds, the girls vanished to their rooms, leaving no trace of their presence apart from one abandoned banner. When the irate Matron entered, there was no one there. The girls giggled from their hiding places.

1942.

Today, I sang at a rally.

Sarojini Naidu was in Madras and I was invited to sing for her. I was in two minds initially about whether to go, and I would never want to put Appa's job at risk, but in the end, I felt he would have no objections. The letter had come addressed specifically to me, asking specially for me, to sing 'Bhartiya' songs for Mrs. Naidu and I felt honoured. It would be an opportunity to serve her and meet her. I have read of her inspirational work for so long now. Why would anyone object to patriotic songs about our country?...

Of course I went. I was very nervous. I've performed on the radio, and in smaller 'kucheris,' but never in front of such a large group and with such a large purpose. I wore my 'khadi' saree, with the national colours in the border, and took my place on the stage. And once I started singing, I lost track of the size of the gathering and where I was.

I will never forget this day!

> ### Bharatiyar
> Chinnaswami Subramania Bharathi, popularly known as Bharathiyar, was a pioneer of Tamil poetry. Many of his passionate songs were written for and adopted by the independence movement.

Over the next few years, Vijaya was invited to sing for a number of leaders of the freedom struggle, including TT Krishnamachari. She even attended prayer meetings organized by Mahatma Gandhi and lectures by Jawaharlal Nehru, always wearing her khadi sari, but made it a point to sit in the back and just listen. She never moved to the front of the audience or drew special attention to herself. Her music was her contribution to the movement.

Vijaya's family, like many in her social circle, were in a unique and conflicted position. Many of them, educated in the British system, and sometimes even educated in England, held important government jobs. This made them employees of the ruling British Government, and it was difficult to associate themselves with the freedom struggle. At the same time, their personal loyalties were strong, and they wanted to fight for an independent India.

For women, the situation was even trickier. Chennai was a relatively conservative society at that time, and involvement in political movements of any kind was risky to a woman's reputation.

Still, many young women from institutions like Queen Mary's College and Women's Christian College took to the streets, participating in protests and chanting 'Inqilab Zindabad'.

Dr TN Vijayalakshmi (1943–1955)

Finally, after so many delays and roadblocks and false starts, Vijaya enrolled in Madras Medical College in 1943. At that time, it was a three-year initial programme, and free for girls. There were around fifteen other women in her class, though no women instructors at that time. Her father was asked, 'Is she a brainiac or is she a flirt? Those are the only two qualifications for a girl to get into that college.' In this case, Vijaya was a brainiac, and had been all her life.

She was determined to learn everything about all forms of medicine. She would show up at the out-patient department at 6 a.m., bright-eyed and bushy-tailed, and insist on being part of all the procedures. She took no holidays during this time and earned herself the nickname Nosy Poker from her seniors, because of her tendency to just show up for all lectures, any lectures, even theirs. Whether it was a weekday or a Sunday, Vijaya would be there in her saree, with her hair pinned up and her notebook open, ready to soak it all in. She was like a human sponge with nose rings.

Her dedication paid off. Unlike the other students, who were told to sit in the gallery and observe during surgery, Vijaya was soon allowed to scrub in and

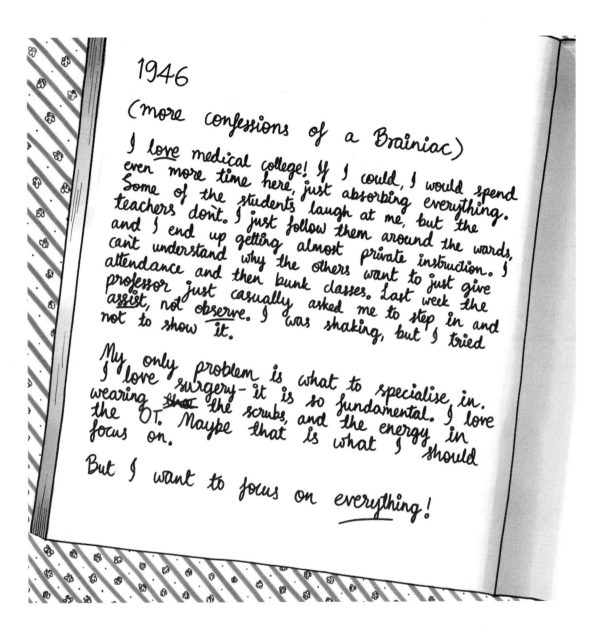

1946

(more confessions of a Brainiac)

I <u>love</u> medical college! If I could, I would spend even more time here, just absorbing everything. Some of the students laugh at me, but the teachers don't. I just follow them around the wards, and I end up getting almost private instruction. I can't understand why the others want to just give attendance and then bunk classes. Last week the professor just casually asked me to step in and assist, not observe. I was shaking, but I tried not to show <u>it</u>.

My only problem is what to specialise in. I love surgery - it is so fundamental. I love wearing ~~that~~ the scrubs, and the energy in the O.T. Maybe that is what I should focus on.

But I want to focus on <u>everything</u>!

assist in actual surgeries. She went far beyond the theory, and observed medicine directly from some of the greatest teachers in the college.

In 1947 Vijaya won the first prize for general surgery from the Medical College. It was also a historic year for the country.

1947, August.

Today, we won Independence.

I didn't venture out of the house much. We were not sure if it was safe. From our buildings, we could hear the crowds outside as they marched past. "Swatantra", "Jai Hind", "Satyameva Jayate", they kept chanting. Everywhere, there's chanting and music. The city music sabhas were already celebrating the centenary of Thiagaraja, and now from every corner we can hear Bharatiyar songs on loud-speakers. On the radio, I heard the speeches and the commentary about the flag hoisting in Delhi, and then the lovely tones of MS* in the evening. We all wore the National Colours.

Independent India!

Independence celebrations in South India

14 and 15 August, 1947 in Madras were largely filled with celebrations, processions and music. Political prisoners who had been imprisoned for participating in the movement were set free and there were joyful reunions. Unlike the north of India, Madras (Chennai, as it is now known) didn't receive very many refugees from partitioned Pakistan. The new tri-colour flag was hoisted at the flagpole in Fort St. George.

MS Subbalakshmi (fondly known as MS), winner of the Bharat Ratna, Ramon Magsaysay Award and Sangeet Natak Academy Award, was a pioneer and shining star of the Carnatic music world. A child prodigy, she gave her first music performance at the age of 11. Very unusually for a young woman of the time, she chose both her own career and her husband, and went on to become one of India's most respected cultural ambassadors. Her fans included Mahatma Gandhi, JN Nehru and Sarojini Naidu. MS and Vijaya's families met often, given their passion for Carnatic music, and were close family friends. MS once even gave an impromptu performance at Vijaya's cousin's wedding.

Dr Vijayalakshmi Ramanan (1948–1955)

In 1948, when Vijaya graduated from medical college to become an intern, she was awarded the prestigious Balfour Memorial Medal. There were benefits to being a brainiac! After so many years of hard work and focus, she carried her medical degree with enormous pride. She then worked for a few years as an intern, and when it was time to select a specialization, she turned again to Dr K.S. Viswanathan for guidance. She chose obstetrics and gynaecology, and in 1953, she became an honorary assistant surgeon.

Vijaya felt extremely grown up and accomplished. With her new medical degree and specialization, she decided to do something even more unusual – though maybe for Vijaya, that was the norm.

The guiding mentor

Vijaya's mentor, Dr K.S Viswanathan, was distantly related to her family. He did his MPH (Masters in Public Health) at Harvard Medical School in the 1930s, and then returned to India to practice medicine. Dr Viswanathan served for many years as the Director of Public Health in Madras, and joined the WHO in Calcutta (Kolkata), before retiring in the 1950s. He provided Vijaya with a powerful role model of public service, while mentoring and supporting her work through her career.

Rather than joining someone else's practice, Vijaya decided to set up her own clinic. She had no idea how to be an entrepreneur or how to run a business, but, as always, she was excited by the opportunity to control her own career. The clinic wasn't much more than a room with a curtain through the middle as a partition, and her helper from home worked as a medical assistant, but it was hers to run, and she paid a monthly rent of Rs 40 to call it her own.

She soon realized that there was much more to running a clinic than having a degree in medicine – she needed to learn how to make money from her skills. And unfortunately, she had no idea how to. While she was able to treat her patients, she struggled to ask them for payment. And often, out of kindness, she wouldn't take any payment from poorer women. She knew she was doing the right thing as a doctor, but as a businesswoman she was failing miserably.

1955 was a very difficult year. In February, Vijaya's father passed away. She was low and dispirited, and struggling to run an independent practice.

And then one day, returning from a patient visit, she found an official-looking envelope on her clinic desk. Tearing it open, she found a letter from her husband-to-be, Staff Captain KV Ramanan.

All those years after that brief encounter, Vijaya and Ram had stayed in touch, become friends and medical professional peers, and recently she had agreed to marry him.

Vijaya didn't need any time to think about the suggestion. She jumped

at the opportunity to do something new – Ram was right, she was ready for a change. Vijaya applied and was called to Delhi for her interview in April 1955, and soon after, she received another official looking letter from the Army Medical Corps (the first of many, as she entered an official life).

She was appointed as a Short Service Commissioned Officer, along with her posting orders. Vijaya was to report to the Air Force headquarters in Delhi on 1 August 1955.

Afterwards, people asked her if she was excited about joining the services and the start of a new adventure. But there were too many things weighing her down then, in April 1955. Vijaya was still grieving the recent loss of her father, her greatest supporter. And she was nervous about everything the new life would bring. No one in her immediate family had joined the Armed Forces before – she had no idea what the services would be like. She had lived in a girls' hostel, and then after that as a day-scholar once her parents moved to Madras. Although she had studied and worked in a man's profession, her life had been very protected so far. She felt unsure of what life would be like on a base, surrounded by men. But she moved forward, confident that her father would have approved of her decision to enter a life of service.

Entry into the Armed Forces in those days (and now) was through a process called a Short Service Commission – rather like a contract to work for the Armed Forces for a period of 10 years. For men, after this 10-year period of serving in the Armed Forces, there was a choice to retire from the Services or apply for a Permanent Commission – in other words a long-term job. The word 'Service' and 'serving' in the Armed Forces clearly showed that working in the Armed Forces wasn't considered a job, it was considered a way of serving the country.

Officer 4971 (1955–1968)

Soon after joining, Vijaya, like her husband-to-be, was seconded (transferred) from the Army to the Air Force. And, just like that, Vijaya made history – she became the first commissioned woman officer to the Indian Air Force.

Between August 1955 and May 1956, Vijaya was stationed in Delhi, waiting for her first posting. In February 1956, she got married to Staff Captain KV Ramanan. Finally, in May, Vijaya was posted to the Jalahalli station in Bangalore.

May, 1956.

Who would've thought that a uniform could cause so much debate?! After much back and forth on what I should wear, we have all finally agreed on the colour of my saree and the length of my sleeves. The material they first sent me was too delicate, so I substituted the Kashmiri silk with a more robust Bangalore silk. At first, they insisted that I wear full-sleeves. But how would that work for a surgeon and a gynaecologist? I wrote back many times, urging them to rethink their decision. They've finally agreed now to three-fourth sleeves, and when required, I plan to fold the sleeves up for better mobility. I never thought when I joined the services that I would also become a costume designer! I think I should stop negotiating now— if I'm not careful, my colleagues warn me, the Air Force will decide to make the blouse sleeveless! (As it is, I'm surprised that they've allowed me to keep my nose rings, so I shouldn't draw more attention to my attire). But I'm happy with what we finally have as a uniform, and I can now change out of my 'civvies'. Last year this time I had no idea what that even meant. Last year this time I didn't even know there were 3 branches in the armed services!

Vijaya was the Duty Medical Officer (DMO) at 2 Airforce Hospital in Jalahalli from 1956 to 1960. It took the staff on base a while to get used to her as DMO. And while the staff got used to a lady DMO, Vijaya got used to a life in the services. She saw patients through the day, both from 2 Airforce Hospital, and those sent across from Command Hospital in the centre of Bangalore. At night she was often on call.

Her two children were born while they were stationed in Jalahalli, and soon after, her husband was transferred to

Kanpur. Vijaya and the children stayed on in Bangalore, waiting for her posting orders.

In 1960, she and the children managed to re-unite with Dr KV Ramanan in Kanpur, but that proved to be short-lived. Soon, her husband was transferred back to Bangalore. By that time, Vijaya's father-in-law, who had also been her guide during medical college, retired, and they moved in with her and the children to supervise them while she worked. In 1962, she and the whole family were moved to Secunderabad. She worked there for six years, and her husband moved back and forth, spending time with the family whenever his posting

permitted. Supported by her in-laws, Vijaya shuttled between home and hospital, and her children grew up happily on various Air Force bases across the country. It was a busy, fulfilling time for Vijaya. She was often tired, juggling home and work, but at the same time she felt lucky to have such a full career.

In 1962, during the India-China war, all the injured soldiers could not be accommodated in the hospitals in the north and often had to be moved for further treatment. Very often the medical staff in Secunderabad worked through the weekend as part of their war effort. Like everyone else, Vijaya pitched in, taking on more hours and more responsibility managing things.

Later, Vijaya was put in charge of running the Medical Board, another serious administrative responsibility. The Medical Board was responsible for Medical categorisation – certifying fitness for service, retirement or the amount of pension someone was to receive. This was an important appointment, and Vijaya took it on with enthusiasm. She found that she always thrived in administrative roles – it was her inherent sense of organisation and structure.

While the children were young, and especially during her time in Jalahalli, Vijaya took a short break from music. But the passion was too strong to ever give up, and she kept looking for a way to bring music back into her life. As soon as she was able to, she resumed performing. From Kanpur, she travelled to Lucknow to perform for AIR; through her years in Secunderabad she performed; and back in Bangalore she returned to her kutcheris. Music always gave her a sense of joy and balance.

Somehow, even with the night shifts and the children and the administrative responsibilities, Vijaya kept her music alive.

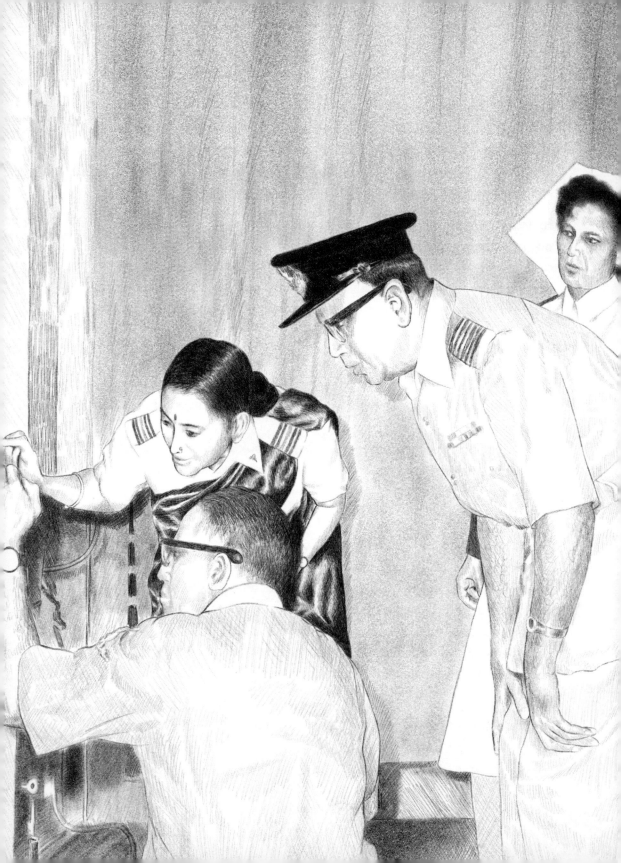

Major Dr V Ramanan (1968–1979)

In 1967, Vijaya was promoted to the rank of Major, the first lady major in Short Service Commissions. In 1968, the IAF took over Command Hospital (Bangalore) from the Army, and Major Dr V Ramanan was part of the advance group that moved to Command Hospital to get things in order.

Again, she was given additional management responsibilities. This time, she was put in charge of the Medical Stores. Traditionally, this was the job of a male officer – it called for stock-taking of medicines, beds, linens and estimating requirements. People were unsure if Vijaya would be able to handle the job but in a few months, she had the hospital running efficiently and well-stocked. She enjoyed managing things. And proving people wrong.

Command Hospital became Vijaya's home and her longest posting. She was based there from 1968 to 1979, when she retired. In April 1971, Vijaya lost her husband. While he was still sick, Vijaya had finally applied for Permanent Commission, and after all the years of hard work and service, the Air Force came through for her instantly. Her application was taken by hand, on a plane, to Delhi, and she was almost immediately granted a Permanent Commission. A few days later, her husband passed away. The Permanent Commission essentially meant that Vijaya could work in the IAF till she retired. After all these years, it was the only life she knew, anyway.

Wing Commander Dr V Ramanan (VSM) 1977

In the 1977 Republic Day Parade, Vijaya became Wing Commander Dr V Ramanan (VSM), when she was awarded the Vishist Seva Medal. She was only the second woman to be given this award, the first being

Flight Lieutenant Dr Padmavathy Bandhopadhyay, who was in fact one of her students.

'For her single minded devotion to duty and organizing medical services for ladies and children of the defence services personnel attending Air Force Hospital, Bangalore, Wing Commander (Mrs.) Vijay Lakshmi Ramanan is awarded Vishisht Seva Medal,' read the Gazette of India Notification Date: 26 January 1977. It was an incredibly proud moment for Vijaya and her family. When she had started off on this journey, she had had no idea what was in store for her, or where it would take her. And now she was being recognized in front of her peers and country for her service.

Wg Cdr Ramanan receiving VSM from Air Chief Marshal Moolgaokar

The last few years had been difficult and sad on many levels, but Vijaya wore her medal with honour.

The Recognition

The Vishist Seva Medal is awarded to Armed Forces Personnel, to recognize 'distinguished service of an exceptional order'. It is awarded by the President of India.

Vijayam maami (1979–2020)

In 1979, Vijaya retired from the services, but not from medicine. She settled down in Bangalore, and revived her early ambition. She started her own clinic again, aiming to serve the poorer patients in Bangalore. As always, she couldn't sit still or do just one thing. During the day she ran the clinic and went on patient calls. In the mornings and evenings, she taught music. She was often seen driving around the city in her little vintage car, either running errands or visiting friends and family. And at home, she spent time with her growing grandchildren and elderly mother-in-law and cooking for guests. Vijaya couldn't imagine slowing down, doing less or having anyone look after her. She had been independent her entire adult life.

Vijaya continued to practice medicine till 2004, when she was 80 years old, and she finally felt that maybe it was time to retire. She reluctantly closed down her clinic, but held firm to her own house in central Bangalore. Her music classes and concerts still kept her busy.

For many years she lived peacefully, relatively unknown, enjoying her time with her growing family.

Yesterday, I was interviewed by a television journalist, for an Independance Day special programme. It has been a funny, surprising year. Suddenly everyone wants to interview me and ask me about my years of service. Maybe it's my age. Such a sweet young girl. She spent so much time with me, listening to my stories. It gave me an excuse to bring out all the photos and look at them - so much fun!

She looked at my medals, my uniform, my old photos. It brought the memories rushing back. The first day on the forces. My CO. My team. The bases we moved to as a family - Secunderabad, Kanpur, Bangalore.

She asked me a few times about the work and the sacrifices, but I don't remember any of that. I remember the joy of being selected the first lady short service commission officer. I remember the glamorous Air Force parties, and after the parties my colleagues accompanying me home so I could reach safely. I was so nervous to be working in close quarters with only men. And in the end, it was so comfortable. I remember the midnight calls from the hospital, and running with the ayah, pushing the trolley together. I remember teaching the young men and women in AFMC. I remember feeling useful, providing service, managing house and hospital. If I could put on my uniform again now and serve, I would, just because of the happiness of those memories. I felt so useful.

The young journalist asked me some funny questions. She was surprised that I still file my own taxes. Why is that surprising? If I don't manage my own accounts and do my own taxes, who will? I might be 94, and I don't have the energy that I used to, but I have complete control of my faculties and my memory. This must be because of my music.

Then she asked whether I think young women should serve in the armed forces. Of course, they should. Everyone who has the mental make-up and discipline should serve. Appa always said – Service before Self.

Of course, things are so different for these younger generations of girls. They have so many ways to serve. Not just in the hospital, I believe now they even have the option of becoming fighter pilots.

If that was possible in my time, would I have become a pilot with the Air Force? I don't know....

On 18 October 2020, Vijaya passed away peacefully in her Bangalore home. She was surrounded by family members, music, books and photos.

Wg. Cdr. Dr (Mrs) Vijayalakshmi Ramanan (VSM) had many titles. But that was only fair – she had accomplished many things. She worked quietly and consistently her entire life, never really thinking of herself as being a trailblazer, but just as someone doing a job. She did things that were unheard of for a woman of her generation, but with a calm confidence and competence. Her career paved the way for a number of pioneering women to join the Armed Forces in different roles. Till 1992, this role was limited to the medical corps; after that, women were allowed to enter as regular officers in aviation, logistics and engineering cadres.

There are currently about 1900 women in the Indian Air Force, serving in multiple capacities.

In 2019, Wing Commander Shaliza Dhami became the first woman flight commander in the Indian Air Force. In 2020, the Indian Air Force announced that the squadron which will fly the newly acquired Rafale jets will include a female pilot.

CADET 001

PRIYA JHINGAN

CADET 001 – PRIYA JHINGAN
The girl who wanted it so badly

It all began with a newspaper advertisement. A very ordinary newspaper advertisement. The type the Indian Army used to put out regularly. But this ad made a young girl in Himachal Pradesh think. It made her wonder. It made her question. And then it made her write a letter. A letter that changed the face of the Indian Army.

The naughtiest girl in school

Priya Jhingan was born in scenic Shimla, surrounded by mountains and fruit orchards. She was the middle of three very close siblings. Her father was a police officer and a part of the Indian Police Services and her mother was a very busy homemaker. Growing up in Shimla felt to her almost like being in an Enid Blyton book. Her younger brother and his friends were her constant companions, and she automatically took charge of their renegade troops. When they were not in school, they were outdoors, all the time. They climbed trees, ropes, mountains, went on long treks, played in streams and built fires to bake potatoes. Sometimes

they sneaked into other people's orchards and climbed the trees to pluck fruit, giggling and running away when they thought they might get caught.

Priya lived two different lives, though. During the day, she studied at Loreto Convent Tara Hall, where the Irish Sisters did their best to instill a sense of decorum in her. It almost never worked. If there was ever anyone in class making the other girls giggle, or playing a prank on the teachers, it was Priya. She was even made to sit separately, in front of the rest of the class, to prevent her from distracting her classmates. After one particularly naughty incident where she was caught throwing burrs (small seeds or fruits with hooks) on a teacher's sweater, Priya

was even stripped of her Captain rank. But she took the punishment on the chin, and continued in her light-hearted pursuit of fun.

Maybe because of this, she was very popular amongst the other students, and even the nuns found it difficult to stay angry with her for long. 'Priya Jhingan,' her teacher, Sister Brenda, once proclaimed in exasperation, 'you are the naughtiest girl in school!' Priya wore that title almost as a badge of pride.

The years passed uneventfully, but even as she grew older, Priya didn't have a clear sense of what she wanted to do when she graduated. No one in her class did. It was still a time before internet access and global exposure. For Priya and her classmates, there were limited role models and most of the time they weren't even aware of the options out there. As Priya grew older though, she started to understand the kind of opportunities her parents had given her. One thing was clear to her – with all the support and investment in her education, she knew that she would find a career one day.

Priya's father was deeply respected in their community – he was known to be an officer of great professionalism and integrity. And he was Priya's hero. She wanted to be like him, dress like him and work like him. Often, when he came home from work, she would take his cap and belt, put on a pair of trousers and a shirt, and pretend to be a police officer. At that time, one of the hit shows on Doordarshan was *Udaan*, a TV show about the trials and challenges of Kanchan Choudhury Bhattacharya, India's second female IPS (Indian Police Service) officer. In those days, there was only one TV channel, and the entire family would watch it together in the evenings. Like the rest of India, Priya's family gathered in front of the TV after dinner every week to watch *Udaan*, and Priya was inspired. One way or another, she was certain she was going to wear a uniform and serve. She knew she had a mission, a calling somewhere. She was just trying to figure out what that could be.

Kanchan Chaudhary Bhattacharya was the second female Indian Police Service officer in India. The first was another inspirational woman leader, Lt. Governor Kiran Bedi. A 1973 batch IPS officer, Ms. Bhattacharya, like Priya, was from Himachal Pradesh. Through her time in the Police Services, she broke gender barriers, and finally made history in 2004 when she was appointed as the first woman DGP (Director General of Police) of the country. Previously, she had also served as an Inspector General with the CISF. She led the Uttarakhand police force between 2004 and 2007. In 1997, she was awarded the President's police medal for her distinguished service. She also received the Rajiv Gandhi award for Excellent All-Round Performance. Ms. Bhattacharya retired on 31 October 2007 after 33 years of service to the country and various states. She was a role model for bravery and service.

Slowly, her ambition started becoming clearer. In the eighth standard, when Priya and her class were asked to write about their future careers, Priya wrote an essay about becoming a Sipahi. She wrote it almost flippantly, without really thinking. And then promptly forgot about it.

Then one day, when Priya was in the ninth standard, the Governor visited her school as the chief guest for a function. He was accompanied by his ADC. An aide-de-camp or ADC is the personal assistant to a high-ranking official in the Army or government service. It is considered a position of great honour.

The ADC was tall, with military-straight bearing, and looked incredibly smart in his official uniform. The girls were so taken with him, they could hardly focus on the Governor's speech. After he left, the girls went back to class buzzing with excitement, and all saying the same thing, 'When I grow up, I want to marry an Army officer.'

Priya felt differently. 'When I grow up,' she declared confidently to her friends, 'I want to *become* an Army officer.'

She finally knew her destination … she just didn't know how to get there.

The long and winding path

For a long while Priya didn't know what to do about her ambition. And when she told her family, they were puzzled. They had always expected her to do something in service—maybe join the IPS like her father—but the Army? How was that possible? 'Women don't join the Army.'

Priya didn't know how to join the Army. She didn't even know anyone in the Army. Nevertheless, she was determined to get there.

After graduating from school, for lack of any other clear plan, Priya started doing her undergraduate course in English. Again, the years passed uneventfully, peacefully. But for Priya the uncertainty grew; she was still searching. This time she was clear what she wanted to

Priya's family was both right and wrong in their belief that women didn't join the Army. While it was true that at that point women hadn't joined the Army as cadets or officers, there was a much longer history of women joining the Army in the medical cadre – as nurses first, and then doctors. Women in the medical cadre were even eligible for Permanent Commission—the equivalent of a long-term job—by this time. Equally importantly, women had been crucial members of the armed services for decades even before that, as the wives and partners of serving soldiers.

do with her life, she just wasn't sure how to achieve it. To pass the time, she learnt martial arts. Not surprisingly for the time, she was the only girl in the Taekwondo class, but it became an outlet for all her physical energy, and she went on to win a gold in the district championship.

One day, when she was in her final year at college, Priya saw an advertisement in the newspaper. The Indian Army was calling for applicants for all cadres. Young men between the ages of 17.5 and 21 were encouraged to apply and experience a life of service and adventure.

Priya read it once. Then again. Why, she started wondering. Why only men? Why not women? Why not me?

She decided to do something. It was the only thing she could think of. The advertisement had provided a contact address. Finally, she had a way to contact the Army. Without even knowing who the Chief of Staff of the Army was, she wrote:

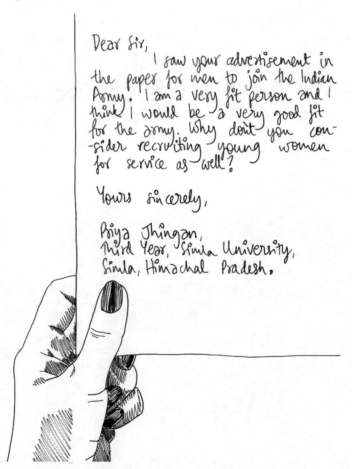

Dear Sir,
    I saw your advertisement in the paper for men to join the Indian Army. I am a very fit person and I think I would be a very good fit for the army. Why don't you consider recruiting young women for service as well?

Yours sincerely,

Priya Jhingan,
Third Year, Simla University,
Simla, Himachal Pradesh.

Priya posted her letter and then waited. She didn't really expect a reply. But at least she felt like she had done everything she could. Two weeks passed, and just as she was starting to believe that her letter had disappeared into some Army black hole, an envelope appeared in the post. Stiff, formal, official and addressed to her.

Dear Ms. Jhingan, I was very happy to receive such an enthusiastic letter from you. Your request for women recruits is in the pipeline. It will happen soon, and I do hope you will apply at that point.

Gen S.F. Rodrigues
Chief of Staff

Priya was relieved. The Army had heard her request and they were going to do something about it. They were just asking her to wait. The question was – how long was she supposed to wait? When would the Army be ready for her? She was already 20, and felt very worried about time running out.

She did a little more research and found out that for law graduates, the Army would accept cadets until the age of 26. This would give her a longer window of opportunity. The decision was simple – she would study law. Her parents had always been completely supportive of her education and ambitions, but privately, they didn't really believe that the policy would change in time for Priya. They weren't at all convinced that she would be able to join the Army, so when she chose law, they were relieved. Law was a steady, dignified career option for a young woman, and her father fully encouraged her decision. So Priya studied law at Himachal University for two years, and she waited. First patiently, and then, as her graduation approached, anxiously.

Graduation came and went, and Priya was now a qualified lawyer. But still there was no news from the Army. Time was running out. Priya started to really worry now. Left with no other choice, she registered with the Himachal High Court, and started practicing law. For six months she went to court and went to work, still waiting and watching. And then one morning, sitting on her balcony, reading the paper, she saw it.

An advertisement in the paper for the WSES – Women Special Entry Scheme. The Army was soliciting female recruits! There it was. The Army was ready for her. And they were calling out to her!

Breathlessly, she read through the advertisement again. The Army was calling for 25 women cadets from across India. Out of those 25 spots, there were two in the Judge Advocate General's Corps (JAG). Only two.

Jumping up, she sprinted with the newspaper across the town to the school where her sister was a teacher, and excitedly pointed at the advertisement.

'It's here,' she managed to say. 'The Army. They're recruiting women. But only two spots in JAG.'

Her sister read the ad, looked at Priya, and then smiled and said, 'I wonder who will get the other spot?'

The application process was quite simple. She filled out the form, sent the application off, and then, once again, began to anxiously haunt the mailbox. She later found out that there were thousands of applicants that year. The Army was inundated. Across India, young women like Priya were drawn to the idea of service and adventure.

Day after day passed, and there was no news. Priya started devising little games in her head. If she wore the same socks as she had on the day of the application, she would hear back that day. If she saw the postman before 11 a.m., she would hear back. Fourteen long, distracted days, and finally she got the call.

Priya was called to the Service Selection Board (SSB) in Allahabad. There were clear instructions about how to get there and what to do. It was Priya's first time travelling alone, and the night before she left, her parents didn't sleep from anxiety. Priya didn't sleep either, but for other reasons. The Army had called her. She was finally doing it. It was going to be an enormous adventure.

She took the train from Shimla to Allahabad. At the station, a bus was waiting to take all the applicants to the Army Centre. There were four days of screening, multiple rounds of tests and a variety of challenges. The applicants were thrown into unknown territories with hurdles and physical challenges. They were tested on their ability to lead teams, creatively use resources like rope, wood and stones, work in teams to create escape strategies and use their bodily strength. It was like playing a very intense, real-life adventure game. All of that mountain-climbing, trekking and apple-plucking finally came in handy – Priya easily sailed through all the physical challenges.

And then, once more, Priya's patience was tested as she waited. She had made a number of friends at Allahabad, and from them she heard that the acceptance letters—or Call letters, as they were known—had started going out. But nothing had come to her yet, and Priya had a last few days of doubt. Finally, one of her new friends offered to go to the Army headquarters in Delhi and look at the list on her behalf. Priya waited nervously at home for the phone to ring.

Officer in training (Chennai OTA)

After the Call letter, she was given a fortnight to get ready. Priya was buzzing with excitement. She took the family's largest suitcase and started packing everything she could think of. She even packed some of her mother's sarees. She had heard that life in the Army was very formal. There might be ballroom dancing, and she would need a saree! Her parents, always supportive of their children's ambitions, helped with planning, logistics and tickets.

One day, about a week before she was scheduled to leave, she was in her room upstairs, packing. She heard her parents talking quietly in their room below, and it suddenly struck her that this was final. Priya shut herself in the bathroom, and cried. She was actually leaving. It would be her first time living outside of home and Himachal. And maybe her last time living at home.

Officers Training Academy
Chennai, —1992

Dear Didi,
          So my adventures have already
begun. Maasi must have told you about
the journey from Simla to Delhi. I just
hopped off the bus for a second and
somehow I managed to sprain my ankle!
It was quite painful, but Maasi and I
managed to make it to Delhi and to the
train station.
I met a number of other lady cadets at the
station, all ready to go to Chennai as well. The
two girls from Delhi are Richa Sharma and
Varsha Mohan. We had good fun on the train
journey - we had each other for company, and
Richa's Maasi had packed so many snacks, we
were munching throughout. We had our comp-
-artment completely to ourselves and every
time we met someone on the train, we
told them we're going to join the Indian
Army. I don't think many of them believed
us!
After two full days - I've seen so much of
India now, from the windows of my compart-
-ment - we reached Chennai and got onto
the Army bus to get to the training
academy.

I thought that after two days rest on the train my ankle would be fine. As soon as we got there, our in-charge, Captain Behl, met us and had us escorted to our quarters, where we left our things. Then we were called for our first briefing. You won't believe what happened then. I was standing in front of the table with the other new cadets, and then suddenly I started to feel light-headed. It must have been the ankle and the weather - they told us Chennai will be hot and humid, but you have to experience this to understand what it means! I kept telling myself to just hold on, just stand up, just focus. But I wasn't able to, and there, in my first briefing, I fainted! It was so embarassing, Didi. I don't know what the Army officers thought of me. Do they now think that all women cadets faint all the time? Or that I am weak and unfit for service?

Everyone was very kind, and I took a short rest and then felt better. But still very embarassed. Training starts tomorrow. I'd better perform extra well, or the Army will think they made a mistake!

The OTA property is really large and I saw some of the grounds today. The male cadets have already been training here for 3 months.

I'm going to bed now- apparently a Rouser will wake us up at 04:45 am tomorrow! They told us about our daily schedules for the next few months. It looks very hectic - and no ballroom dancing it appears!
My uniform is a little big and not a good fit, but I'm so excited to wear it. I'll send some photos when I can.
I'll write again soon.

Love,
Priya.

The new women cadets spent 6 months at the OTA. On their very first day, their Officer-in-Charge, Captain TS Behl, said, 'From now onwards expect to be dealt with as an officer, not a woman cadet.' The message was clear – the Army would be making no concessions for them on training. Neither the Army nor the cadets really knew what to expect during that first training period. Everything was being tested for this first set of cadets and no one was sure what their endurance levels would be. At first, instead of handing the women the standard, heavy 7.62mm rifle, they handed them canes. Of course, the women protested, and soon they were practicing with regular rifles just like the other cadets.

Today we got a beauty parlour on campus! I'm sure you're wondering why that's such exciting news, but to us it is ex--citing. Till now they didn't have one! All the officers' wives go off the campus to get their work done. But we have no time. We still have to wear those embarassingly short shorts for drills, but at least we don't have to parade our hairy legs for everyone!

Fortunately, Mrs. Behl understood our problem immediately and helped us raise a request. The OTA higher-ups were sur--prised but very helpful immediately. And now, here we are - we can finally do our eyebrows again! I'm not sure if the next batch of women will even under--stand what a great victory this is!

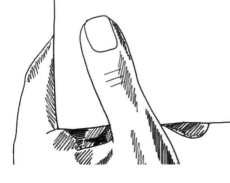

The next few months at OTA were gruelling and intense. Priya, along with the other cadets, got up at 4.45 a.m. every day. They spent their mornings on the courts in drills, PT sessions and parades. Then they would change into uniform for breakfast and classes, followed by more drills, exercises and parades, all through till bedtime. They learnt rifle shooting, riding, cycling and swimming. In class they were taught Economics, Tactics, Map-reading and Military History. For Priya, it was her first time in a pool, on a cycle, on a horse – almost everything was new.

Early on during her training, Priya woke up one morning in excruciating pain. Doubled up, she went to consult the medical officer at the OTA, who examined her and said cheerfully that it was just gallstones. He could keep her in the medical centre for a week, but missing so many sessions meant that Priya would not be able to graduate with her batch. She would have to wait and join the next batch. That was it – Priya leapt out of bed and returned to class. Gallstones were not serious – they would eventually get washed out of her system. She would have to live with the pain for a while, because after working so hard to get here, she was determined not to miss her chance to graduate with the rest of the batch. In the meantime, she would just need to manage her pain.

The next day, the new cadets were sent on a run. Priya was worried about how she was going to manage to keep up, given her stomach pain, but she set off like the others. She kept worrying as she kept running. What if she came in last? What if she did so poorly that the Army changed their mind about her? What if she had to take more time off?

After a few minutes she realized none of the others were running next to her. Surprised, Priya turned to look back and saw the rest of the group miles behind her! She had been so stressed and worried, she hadn't even realized that she had long passed the others and was far ahead. That was when it struck her – all her constraints were just in her head. She had all the abilities and opportunities needed. She just needed to ignore the doubts and run. Priya let go, and ran. She won the race by a large margin, and never looked back.

Priya loved everything physical, and after that brief self-doubt she excelled – out of the combined class of 250 cadets, she stood 20th in terms of physical fitness. Being Cadet 001 gave her an added sense of responsibility. Because they were the first batch of women, the Army was testing the abilities and boundaries of the women. Everything they did would set the standards for batches of women to come. And as Cadet 001, Priya was always called upon first to do anything. She felt very strongly about sending the right message about women being ready for the Army.

Six months later, training ended with the traditional Passing Out Parade and Pipping Ceremony. For weeks before, the cadets practiced. On graduation day they would be required to parade on the grounds – their marching, salutes, uniforms, everything had to be absolutely perfect. The authorities were a little apprehensive – would the lady cadet contingent be able to match the Army's very exacting standards? As always, the women rose to the challenge. Their parade was pitch perfect.

All the cadets' families joined them in Chennai for this momentous day, and families had a role to play in the ceremony as well. A key part of the Pipping Ceremony was the attaching of the stars to the epaulette and Priya's parents played their part by pinning the Officer stars on her epaulette. It was a momentous feeling – the last step towards finally, officially being in the Army.

Graduating from OTA

After those tentative beginnings, the OTA in Chennai has been a trailblazer in supporting and preparing women in the Armed Forces. It has hosted and trained numerous other batches of women officers, including almost 500 women officers from other countries (Afghanistan, Kyrgyzstan, Bhutan, Seychelles, Maldives and Uganda).

At the end of the training period, Priya passed with a silver medal and the designation WS002. She and all the other cadets had been recruited under the Women's Special Entry Scheme, and so each of them was given the title WS00_. Captain Behl later told her that he was extremely disappointed. 'If you had just applied yourself a little bit more in the theory classes, you could have been a gold medallist,' he told her. 'You could have been Cadet 001 and WS001.' But for happy-go-lucky Priya, it didn't matter. Despite the intense training schedule, she had loved her time at the OTA, and if she didn't have a gold medal, a silver medal wasn't bad either. She had made some very close friends and she was shortly going to be sent to her first posting in her new Army life.

A month before graduation, she received news of her first posting – Lucknow Command HQ. Deep in her heart, she had hoped the Army would change its mind and allow the posting of women cadets on the field, but it wasn't to be. It was a bit disappointing, but Priya was still excited. After a leave of 21 days, she would take a train to Lucknow— her first time there—and begin her new life as an officer.

While Priya Jhingan and the 24 others were the first set of women cadets in post-Independent India, they were not the first women in India's military history.

Rajalakshmi Sehgal with
Subash Chandra Bose, circa 1942

Captain Lakshmi Sehgal and the Rani of Jhansi regiment

The Rani of Jhansi Regiment was the Women's Regiment of the Indian National Army, founded by Subash Chandra Bose in 1942. The INA was formed to overthrow the British in India and the Rani of Jhansi Regiment was one of the few all-female combat regiments anywhere in the world. Led by Captain Rajalakshmi Swaminathan (Sehgal), it was composed largely of Indian expatriate volunteers from Singapore and Malaysia. The cadets went through military and combat training, with drills and route marches as well as weapons training in rifles, hand grenades, bayonet charges and jungle warfare. Eventually, the INA and the Regiment had to retreat and disband, but not before the regiment had provided valuable support services.

Veeramangai Velu Nachiyar and Kuyili

Rani Velu Nachiyar was the first queen from India to rebel against the British forces in the mid-18th century. While there are a handful of other women warriors and queens who stood out for their military achievements, what makes Veeramangai ('brave woman' in Tamil) Velu Nachiyar exceptional is that she took the unusual step of raising, training and successfully deploying an all-woman Army —the Udaiyal Army—in combat against the British forces. The name of the Army was itself a tribute to Udaiyal, a brave village girl who resisted the British Army. Equally notable was the female Commander-in-Chief of the Udaiyal Army, Kuyili. On 31 December 2008, the Indian Post released a commemorative stamp of Velu Nachiyar.

Officer Jhingan

Dear Didi,

I'm sorry I didn't write before, but again, there was just no time! I have to tell you what happened on the first day I got here. I hadn't changed into my uniform— I was still in my civvies. When I got to the Command HQ gate, full of 'josh' to report for duty, the guard wouldn't let me go through! "Aap andar kahan ja rahe hain?" He thought I was a civilian! I kept saying, "Arre bhai, no. I'm an officer, WS001," but he didn't believe me. I guess the circular hasn't gone around yet to all teams that there is a new batch of women officers in the army. Finally, another officer saw me and I explained what was happening. The guard very grudgingly let me through. It isn't his fault though— everyone here is still getting used to having women officers on the same campus. My living quarters are exactly the same as the others, and the only other woman cadet, posted in Lucknow, Sujatha Pandey, is posted in the ASC unit, not Command HQ, so I don't meet her that often.

Posting to Lucknow Command HQ

Lucknow Command HQ was staffed with a number of senior ranking officials. Second Lieutenant Jhingan definitely stood out in her posting, not just for being a woman, but also for being so junior. It could have been quite intimidating for Priya, but fortunately she was used to being one of the boys, and she quickly made herself comfortable there. There was one small issue: the building had no women's toilet as there were no other women working there full-time! But rather than be embarrassed by the predicament, Priya found ways to manage. She realized that the only way would be to be creative and devise her own strategies.

While many people in the Army were very welcoming to the new batch of Officers, Officer Jhingan also found that not everyone adapted to the idea that quickly.

Everyone here treats me like an equal now. But there's only one problem. Or at least there used to be a small problem but I solved it. Every morning, going through the gates, the soldier at the gate salutes each person going in. "Namaste Sir," "Good morning Sir," "Jai Hind Sahib." Only I got nothing. Day after day. I thought after some time the guards would get used to my presence, which they did. But they were still not ready to salute me. I asked Sujatha if she faced something similar in her posting, and she said yes. She had exactly the same problem, and she had reported it to her CO (Commanding Officer), who then took the fellow to task.

I could have asked my CO to order the guard, but I didn't want to. I wasn't very happy with the idea of forcing him to salute me. I had a better idea!

Yesterday when I walked up to the gate, I saluted the guard first thing, and said, "Jai Hind!" Of course, then he had no choice, and he had to salute me back! "Jai Hind, Sahib." Now I think he's got the message and every day he salutes me, like any other officer, whenever he sees me.

He says "Jai Hind," I say, "Jai Hind" and we pass each other.

Patriotism always wins the day!

While in Lucknow, Priya had to study Military Law. She went through what is known as the Young Officers Course, ending with an examination at the Institute of Military Law, near Nagpur. She topped the course, and was finally ready to practice law in the Army.

The duty of the Judge Advocate Generals group in the Army is to conduct court martials – the legal trials of military officers, as per Military Law and Military protocols.

Dear Didi,

I was so nervous yesterday. After years and years of studying and 'hazaar' courses and exams, yesterday I had to conduct my first court martial. I spent all my time preparing the case, my words, my argument. I ironed my uniform and polished my blacks until they shone. Then, yesterday morning I walked into the courtroom and looked around at the jury. As always, the jury bench had a number of extremely senior rank-ing officials. Apparently, they saw me, and they got even more nervous than me! (Okay, I admit that I'm more petite than the average Judge Advocate here!)

One of the Colonels came up to me and said, "So Lieutenant, you are conducting the court martial today?" "Yes, sir," I said, trying not to sound nervous. "So how many court martials have you conducted so far?" he asked me. My mind was literally racing, Didi. There I was, a petite, girlish woman, conducting my first court martial ever. If I told the court that, I would have lost their confidence completely. And when I saw their doubting faces, I suddenly felt more con--fident than ever— I might be only a Second Lieutenant in that room, but I was the qualified expert on law, I was the one who knows the procedures. I was the Advocate Judge here.

So, I did something that you probably won't like, Didi, but it was my strategy. (And it worked, Didi). I said with a smile, "Colonel, this is my seventh court martial."

I could literally see the entire court relax when I said that. "Oh, then we are in safe hands!"

And the court martial went off very smoothly. I managed the day, wrote up the proceedings, gave them feedback which they took very respectfully and then wound the whole thing up.

When we were done and everyone was shaking my hand, I thought it would be better to come clean. I stood up to make my announcement. The Colonel gave me a wonderful opening, saying, "Thingan, I want to congratulate you on a very well run court martial."

"Actually Sir," I said, "that was my first court martial." His jaw dropped, but after that he took it in very good humour.

And now I know I have arrived. I am no longer a newbie at this job, and it is such a relief!

Priya Jhingan was sometimes still the naughtiest girl in school!

While in Lucknow, Priya was given the opportunity of attaching herself to an infantry division to understand more about the Army. She jumped at the chance, and spent a month with the legendary Garhwal Rifles Regiment, living with them, going through their training, their routines, their parades. It was an extremely special time in her life. She had always wanted to be posted to an Infantry Regiment, and though that could not happen, at least she had a chance to experience the intense Army life.

During her posting there, Priya met a young Captain Malhotra, also posted in Lucknow at that time. He had a dashing motorcycle, and was, like her, one of the youngest officers at Command HQ. They ended up spending a lot of time together.

After two and a half years of intense learning in Lucknow, Priya received notice that she was to be transferred to Calcutta Eastern Command. Captain Malhotra also received a transfer notice – to Nabha, Punjab. They thought about their situation for a while, and then came up with a strategy. Both Captain Malhotra and Lieutenant Jhingan were officers of the Army. It was their duty to go where the Army sent them. There was one thing they could do, though, to stay together.

They got married. They still had to go to their separate postings, but at least now they felt like they were together in some way.

The Travelling Army Life

Through her time in the Army, Priya was successively posted at Lucknow, Calcutta, Ambala and Chennai. But this was just where her house was. She always had a suitcase packed and ready, and as part of her work, she travelled to every nook and corner of the country, conducting court martials. In those ten years, Priya saw more of India than she had ever dreamed of, and she loved every moment of it. Everywhere she went, she met interesting people, experienced new foods and learnt about different cultures.

When Priya Jhingan and that first batch of women cadets joined the Army, they had literally been an experimental batch. The Army wanted to observe them to see how they fared, before extending the opportunity to other women. After graduating from OTA, the entire batch of cadets received their Short Service Commission of five years. Five years later, the Army seemed confident of their abilities and extended the commission for another five years. As her tenth year of service approached, somewhere in her heart, Priya was certain that again, the Army would grant an extension. She had heard that the policy was under discussion somewhere. Unfortunately for Priya, the decision to grant permanent service to women wasn't taken in time for her. In 2002, Major Priya Jhingan's journey in the Army had come to an end, and she realized she would soon have to retire.

Out of the twenty-five cadets recruited in 1992, only seven remained in active service by that time. Life, as she knew it, was going to change again, and Priya was uncertain and more than a little sad. But she was also so dedicated to the services, she didn't think of questioning the decision or railing against the authorities. She had had a fantastic, adventurous time during the last ten years, making deep friendships, travelling the country, meeting her husband and serving the country.

Now there was no choice – the incredible journey was over, and it was time to figure out what to do next.

Army Officer to Army Wife

The first few months after retirement were deeply disorienting to Priya. And also, slightly depressing. She was used to being busy and productive, and even with a small child and a house to run, she needed more. For as long as she could remember, the Army had been Priya's North Star. Without it to guide her choices, she felt a little lost.

She applied for job after job after job, but somehow nobody ever hired her. She started to wonder if something was wrong with her qualifications or abilities.

Even as a young girl, Priya's aspiration hadn't been to be an Officer's wife. After some thought, Priya decided that the only way forward was to be a student again. Since she was already a trained lawyer, she studied and became qualified to practice law in Haryana, where they were posted at the time.

Dear Didi,
Another frustrating day and another frustrating job rejection. This time I really thought it would go through. They did 3 rounds of interviews with me, and I thought that they really liked me. And then today I got a call saying they would not be moving forward. I was so upset I just asked straight, "But why? I thought it was a good interview?" Apparently they thought that because I was a Major, because of my qualifications, I would be too expensive for them! I didn't know how to tell them that I'm not that expensive, really!

But, that was that. Another dead end. And there are only limited job opportunities where we are posted now.

After all those years of studying and learning, how ironic that I'm now unemployable. Sorry, I'm just feeling a little disappointed.

Send me some funny news from school. Or the kids.
            I will write again soon.
                        Love,

                        Priya.

Soon after, though, her husband was transferred to Gangtok, and Priya and their son moved with him. Priya had always enjoyed learning, so in Gangtok she went back to college and this time, got a Bachelor's degree in Journalism and Mass Communications. Then, once again, Priya started afresh, looking for jobs and wondering what to do. In a chance meeting at her son's school, Kendriya Vidyalaya, the Principal suggested that since her English was so good, she talk to the local newspaper. Priya thought she should try it out. She was game to work on something new, so she took an appointment and went to meet the editor of *Sikkim Express*, the local daily newspaper. They had a long, engaging conversation, and before she knew it, Priya found herself in charge of designing and writing for a new weekly magazine, the *Sikkim Express Feminie*.

Suddenly, Major Priya Jhingan was a journalist and editor.

For a year, every Friday, she brought out a small magazine with an interview focusing on The Woman of the Week, restaurant reviews, articles and stories. She enjoyed it immensely, because it also gave her an opportunity to go out and explore the vibrant city they lived in. Priya had always loved meeting new people and being out and about – this job played to all those passions.

Around the same time, the principal of her son's school in Gangtok had another suggestion for her. The principal suggested she try her hand at teaching. Always ready for a challenge, Priya tried that out too. And found that she loved it. She enjoyed the interactions with the students, their energy, their questions. From being the naughtiest girl in school, she had become the teacher in school, and she found the switch surprisingly enjoyable. She had never thought of herself as a teacher—teaching was her sister's expertise—but it came naturally to her as well.

Over the next few years, Priya lived the life of an Army wife. She and her family moved around constantly, following her husband to each posting. Priya kept finding opportunities to learn and do something interesting. She wrote, taught, ran a management centre, conducted lectures on legal rights – in short, she kept very busy. And every day, she continued to run.

Back in the Beautiful Mountains

In 2012, Priya and her family visited the Lawrence School in Sanawar. Her sister was on the faculty there, and they were considering the school for Priya's son.

When they got to Sanawar, the family fell in love with the area. Priya's husband, Lieutenant Colonel Malhotra, had also retired from the Army by now, and the family decided to settle down in Himachal. After years of travelling around India (and even the globe), it felt like a wonderful homecoming for Priya. Being back in the mountains felt right – peaceful, beautiful and filled with opportunities for an outdoor life. It all reminded her of her idyllic childhood. She was ready to settle down – a little.

Priya became an English teacher at Sanawar, and Lt. Colonel Malhotra set up an adventure sports company close by in Solan. Every year, she was the teacher who accompanied the students on their high-altitude treks.

In between, very briefly, Priya got to relive the adventures of her previous life.

Maj. Priya with her sister at the Lawrence School, Sanawar

Khatron Ka Khiladi

In 2013, quite out of the blue, Priya received a call from her old Commander-in-Chief, now Major General Behl. Apparently the organizers of *Fear Factor* India, *Khatron Ke Khiladi*, had been in touch with him. They were launching their first season in India and putting together a group of participants from the armed services. Would Priya be interested?

Priya had only two questions:
'Would any of it be life-threatening dangerous?'
'Would they have to eat creepy-crawlies?'

The answer to both questions was no, and Priya didn't need any more convincing. Like her plunge into the Army, she had no real idea what she was letting herself in for, but that never fazed her. Whatever it was, she was up for it. In fact, she was excited about it!

A month later, Priya joined a team of eleven retired officers in Johannesburg. She was the only woman in the team, and together the group spent twenty-one days in South Africa. Each of the participants was teamed up with a celebrity partner – Priya's was model and actress, Tupur Bannerjee. When the team first arrived in Jo'burg, they were told that the Army Officers would be living in a tented camp, and the women would be hosted in more luxurious chalets. When Priya found out she was expected to stay in the chalets, she protested. This was her last chance to live again like an Army Officer, and she jumped at it. And so, she moved into the tents with her colleagues. It was a deeply fun bonding experience, and Priya loved every single challenge of the show, from picking up rats to retrieving keys from a cockroach-filled jar. She even loved the stunts where she didn't quite succeed, like jumping from one speeding boat to another, both of them racing through the water at 120km per hour. Priya almost made it across, but at the last minute she slipped, let go and fell into the water, getting completely drenched. The most nerve-wracking stunt was one in which a rope was tied between the 17th floor of two buildings, and participants were expected to crawl across.

It was physically challenging and exciting, and Priya got a chance to collaborate again, briefly, with other Army veterans. As with everything else in her life, Priya threw herself headlong into the experience and thoroughly enjoyed the camaraderie and the bonding. At the end of the month, Priya returned to her husband and son completely rejuvenated.

A Life of Adventure

Finally, after many years of teaching, Priya gave that up in 2019 to return to her very first love – outdoor adventure sports. She moved to Solan to help Lt. Col. Malhotra run PepTurf, and now Priya joins her husband as he takes groups skiing, trekking, climbing and rafting. Recently, she completed an exhilarating climb and scaled the peak of Mount Kilimanjaro in East Africa. As long as there are adventures to be had, and peaks to be scaled, Major Priya Jhingan (retired) will find them.

The Women's Special Entry Scheme

In 1992, the Indian Army introduced the experimental WSES on a short term (five-year) basis, throwing open the doors for women to join the Army in the aviation, logistics, law, engineering and executive cadres. It was a real turning point and over the years, 900 women have been recruited annually. Initially introduced as a short-commission, experimental programme, in 2006 the time limit on service was increased to ten years, with a possibility of being extended to fourteen years. It has now been extended to up to fourteen years.

While those initial batches of lady cadets, as they were known, paved the way for future generations of women in the Armed Forces, the men in their regiments had to make an equal amount of adjustment. For the first time, they had to deal with women officers in their training centres and on their bases; as equals and sometimes as commanding officers.

In 2020, the Indian Supreme Court decided that women officers would also now be eligible for permanent commissions across the board, in every area of the Army, including the combat streams – infantry, mechanised infantry, artillery and armoured corps. These streams constitute 70% of the Army. They will be eligible for command posts and also junior command courses that groom them for higher ranks of Army leadership. There are currently about 1600 women in the Indian Army.

Major Priya Jhingan and that entire first batch of the WSES blazed a trail that other women eagerly followed.

6 WOMEN, A BOAT CALLED TARINI
AND AN EPIC JOURNEY

6 WOMEN, A BOAT CALLED TARINI, and an Epic Journey

On 10 September 2017, a boat set off from Vishakhapatnam. The boat was captained by Lieutenant Commander Vartika Joshi and managed by an all-women crew of Naval officers. The six-woman crew was going to attempt to circumnavigate the world. At that point, the Indian Navy wasn't even inducting women as sailors (though they served in other administrative cadres). Their companion on this epic journey was a INSV (Indian Navy Sailing Vessel) INSV *Tarini*, and most fittingly, they were seen off by Nirmala Sitharaman, India's new Minister of Defence.

When they returned to India 254 days, 21,980 nautical miles and many, many adventures later, they had made history. They were India's first all-female crew to circumnavigate the globe.

What is circumnavigation?

For a voyage to be considered a circumnavigation, it must start and end from the same port, cross the three great Capes – Cape Leeuwin (Australia), Cape Horn (South America) and the Cape of Good Hope (South Africa), cross the Equator twice and cover a distance equal to or more than the circumference of the Earth.

History of women circumnavigators

The first woman to circumnavigate the globe was Jeanne Baret (French). Around 1766, Jeanne joined a royal expedition captained by Louis Antoine de Bougainville, disguised as a man. Women were not allowed on Navy ships at the time. The expedition aimed to be France's first circumnavigation of the globe, but it was also meant to collect plant and animal specimens for France and French colonies. Jeanne (or Jean, as she renamed herself) joined the expedition at her employer's request, and with a deep interest in flora and fauna – she had established herself as a herbalist. Even though her identity was discovered along the way, Jean managed to eventually sail her way back to France, and in the process, became the first woman to circumnavigate the globe.

Dame Ellen MacArthur (British) not only solo circumnavigated the globe, but also broke the world record for the fastest solo circumnavigation of the globe, completing the 27,354 nautical mile trip in 71 days, 14 hours, 18 minutes and 33 seconds. She set the record in 2005.

Laura Dekker (Dutch) fought the authorities and broke multiple boundaries when, in August 2010, she set sail on her epic journey onboard her two-masted ketch (a type of sailboat with two sails instead of the usual one) and arrived, 518 days later, at Simpson Bay on St Maarten in January 2012. She had broken the world record for solo circumnavigation. She was also only 16 years and four months old at the time.

The Crew

The Skipper

Vartika Joshi grew up surrounded by the hills. Her parents were educators in Srinagar and Rishikesh, so she and her brother kept moving between the two locations, and went to school in both places. Growing up, she had never even seen the ocean. Both in Rishikesh and Srinagar, she grew up next to rivers (Ganga and Alaknanda) and while they were an intrinsic part of her life, she was afraid of the water. Often, when she went out with her father for a stroll, he would leap into the Alaknanda and start swimming. Vartika preferred what she called 'dry swimming', at a safe distance on the shore.

As a young girl, in fact, Vartika had a very different—and yet very similar—ambition. She wanted to explore the unknown – in this case, space. She wanted to be an astronaut. There was something about space, its vastness and mystery, that she felt drawn to. Space offered her an openness and potential for great adventures, and though she didn't know it at the time, in her heart, Vartika was in search of great adventures, no matter where she found them. Kalpana Chawla was an enormous inspiration through Vartika's school days.

At the same time, TV shows like *Aarohan* were starting to plant tiny little seeds in her mind, without her realizing it.

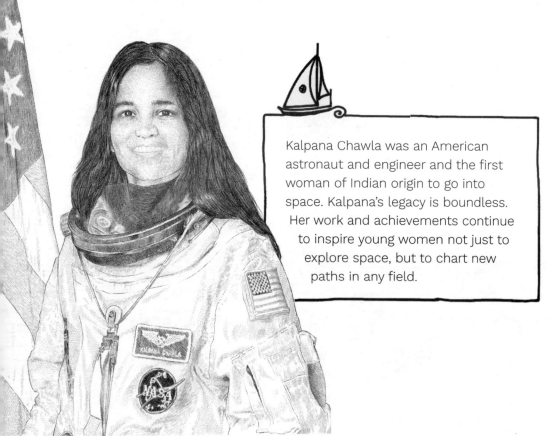

Kalpana Chawla was an American astronaut and engineer and the first woman of Indian origin to go into space. Kalpana's legacy is boundless. Her work and achievements continue to inspire young women not just to explore space, but to chart new paths in any field.

Aarohan was a Doordarshan TV show in the late 1990s, following the lives and adventures of a group of women cadets in training at the Naval Academy. The world it described was ahead of its time, and it inspired many young women like Vartika.

Vartika was an academic girl, always with her head in a book, so it was no surprise to her family when she did well at school and chose to study aerospace engineering in Delhi. She graduated in 2010 with a B-Tech in Aerospace Engineering, and, in landlocked Delhi, was wondering what to do next when an opportunity presented itself. Some Navy officials visited her college as part of a university selection scheme, with a view to identifying new recruits.

Vartika was suddenly filled with a deep curiosity about life out at sea. While she was still terrified of swimming and the water, something perversely made her move towards what was scaring her. Many years ago, Vartika's father had given the Short Service Exam, but somehow had chosen not to pursue a career in the Army. On their many walks together, he had told Vartika about this, and this had intrigued her. Vartika wondered about life in the services, and if that was what she was meant to do.

Vartika had taken the GRE exam recently, and the obvious next step for her would be to go abroad, do a Master's degree and then start working in research. But Vartika chose not to do the obvious thing. Almost without knowing why, and to the surprise of her family, Vartika decided to take the plunge and apply for the Indian Navy. She was the first member of her family to join the Armed Forces, and no one knew what to expect.

Rani Abbakka – the Admiral Queen

While the Indian Navy doesn't currently take women officers on warships, legend (and maybe history) tells us of a warrior queen known as Rani Abbakka, the Admiral Queen of Ullal (close to Mangalore, Karnataka). In the 16th century, Rani Abbakka fought and resisted multiple attacks from the Portuguese, including commanding a number of sea vessels that conducted naval warfare with them. For many centuries, India (and other parts of the world) were under constant attack and invasion by the Portuguese, but Rani Abbakka was able to hold them off. History unfortunately, doesn't document much about her, but in 2009 the Indian Coast Guard launched ICGS *Rani Abbakka*, a Patrol Vessel. The name was specially chosen to showcase a great and forgotten warrior queen.

Naively, Vartika thought that joining the Navy would mean a life at sea. However, at that point the Navy did not recruit women for sea-going platforms. Vartika gave the Short Service Board Exam for the Navy, passed and was selected. She was thrilled. She thought she was now going to sail the seas and explore the world.

Vartika spent the next six months at the Indian Naval Academy in Kochi. She learnt the basics of navigation, seamanship and chartwork. But what she loved the most was the physical, outdoor aspect of her training. All her life Vartika had been a bit of a bookworm. For the first time, she realized how much she enjoyed the outdoors. The time at INA gave her a newfound joy in physical activity and a deep sense of camaraderie with her fellow trainees. She was one of thirty other female recruits in the batch, and all the new recruits were treated alike and expected to train and perform at the same level.

After six months of training, Vartika joined the Naval Construction Cadre as a technical recruit, and went to Visakhapatnam for more specialized training. Then she spent a year and a half at IIT Delhi, getting a Master's degree in Naval Construction. Finally, after all that hard work, training and studying, she was ready for her first appointment.

In 2012, Vartika was posted to Visakhapatnam, where she worked as part of the team designing India's nuclear submarine, *Arihant*. She enjoyed her work and her engineering mind liked the challenge of design and construction. But, something fundamental was missing. When she first found out that female officers in the Navy were not sent out to sea, she had been deeply disappointed. Even after that, she hoped that living by the sea and working in the Navy would be enough, but it wasn't. It felt like after all her years of hard work, she had come so tantalizingly close, but still not close enough.

In Visakhapatnam, Vartika worked twelve hours a day, Monday through Saturday. But every Sunday, she was irresistibly drawn to the Watermanship Training Centre (WTC) in Vizag. This was where she got her first introduction to sailboats. After spending several Sundays there, she had the courage to ask one of the instructors to show her how to use the laser sailboat. He showed her how to rig it up and use the wind for sailing, and then sent her out to practice. That first time by herself on a sailboat, Vartika capsized. And kept capsizing. Until she finally had to be rescued, boat and all, and brought back to shore. But oddly, even the capsizing felt thrilling to her, and Vartika was hooked. From then on, every Sunday she went to WTC Vizag, and spent every free hour there until she had mastered the ability to sail a small laser boat. Once she got the hang of it, the wind and the waves became an addiction. Everything that she had learnt in theory—such as the Bernese theorem of aerodynamic principles—was no longer academic, but real. Vartika didn't know how, but she knew she needed to live a life out at sea. Deep down, she knew there was more adventure to be had in the Navy. She was sure of it, and she could no longer just wait and hope that the adventure would find her. She decided to actively go find it.

A laser is a small single-sail dinghy, designed to be sailed single-handedly. The size and weight mean that it can be operated and managed by one person, but this also puts enormous importance on the skills of that one person.

In 2014, the tide literally turned in Vartika's favour. The Navy decided to form a mixed gender crew for a race – a transatlantic voyage from Rio de Janeiro to Cape Town. Sitting at her desk in Vishakhapatnam, Vartika saw the signal (an official naval notification) go out on her computer, and her world stopped for a moment. This was it. This was what she was waiting for. Vartika volunteered immediately for the voyage, telling her manager about her ambition. It was not smooth sailing though. It took a lot of effort to get approval to be away from her job for the four to five months that were needed for the journey.

Everyone along the way needed convincing. But Vartika was so confident, she pushed it through. She went for the screening in Mumbai and was selected for the three-leg voyage. The plan was that at each of the three legs—Goa, Cape Town and Rio de Janeiro—a female officer would join the existing male crew.

Vartika, the Naval Architect from Uttarakhand, was finally going on her first voyage.

That first voyage was a nightmare. Vartika joined her two male crewmates for the journey from Rio to Cape Town. It was her first voyage, her first time on INSV *Mhadhei*, and her first time out at sea for such an extended period. She didn't know the vessel, she didn't know the basics of long-voyage sailing, and to add to her miseries, the seas were rough, and she was intensely seasick. Vartika, who had looked forward to this experience for so, so long, spent the first few days of her first voyage lying limp and prone on the boat deck, too weak from throwing up to do anything. Her crewmates, Cdr. Satish and Cdr. Bedi, looked after her ably and kindly, even feeding her when she was unable to stand up. After three days, Vartika learnt the secret of overcoming seasickness – engaging her mind productively. She also felt more than a little guilty that the three-member crew was one member short. She forced herself to get up and get busy, and found that it made an enormous difference to how she felt. She had managed to overcome her seasickness.

That particular leg of the journey was dogged by bad luck, though. Only three days out from Rio, the vessel was caught in a massive storm in the Atlantic. They couldn't make headway and the winds took the boat completely off course. The diesel generator stopped working, and with it the pumps. Now there was no running water on the boat. Then the engine broke down as well. The crew had no GPS, no modern forms of navigation and no means of communicating with the shore or their nervous families back home. After spending nineteen days out at sea, the crew had to revert to traditional methods of sailing and make their way back to Brazil.

Those nineteen days showed Vartika what life out at sea was like, without any external support, just living on the basics. It was an eye-opener. It gave her a very real sense of how perilous and difficult life at sea could be, and taught her what every sailor knows – that the sea will not be merciful to you.

It should have turned her off sailing forever. But instead, the opposite happened. Vartika had had a taste of crew camaraderie and the vastness of the ocean. After that voyage, she constantly felt like life on land was bland and missing something.

Back in Vizag, at her regular job, Vartika's mind kept returning to the sea. She knew she had to go back.

In December 2014, when there was a call for women volunteers to join Cdr. Dilip Donde on a celebratory voyage of 100,000 miles, Vartika volunteered again. Once more, there was a period of convincing required, but by now her manager understood that Vartika was happiest and most productive at sea, and so he helped her make her case. In April 2015, Vartika was posted to Goa, and she completed the 100,000 mile voyage with Cdr. Donde. Another female officer volunteer, Pratibha Jamwal, was also part of the crew, and would soon become a core member of Vartika's life.

Crew Feature: Lt. Cdr. Pratibha Jamwal

Pratibha Jamwal grew up in Kullu Valley, another mountain girl. She was quiet and studious and won scholarships throughout her schooling in her home village, Mohal. Growing up in Himachal, there was always the lure of the uniform, but when Pratibha thought about serving, it was always the Army. Being so far from the sea meant that the Navy wasn't even an idea in her head, let alone an ambition. But life happened, and instead of joining the Army, Pratibha found herself doing what so many other smart young women were doing across India – joining an Engineering college. It was while she was in Baddi, studying Communication and Electronic Engineering, that she came across an intriguing opportunity. The Navy visited her college to make a presentation, and Pratibha attended the talk. Suddenly she learnt

about a completely new opportunity for her career, and new horizons opened up. Pratibha took an unusual decision – she decided to apply to the Indian Navy.

The Service Selection Board has always been an extremely difficult and rigorous selection exam, and like all the others, Pratibha found it challenging. Her final selection was in Bangalore, and when Pratibha left home for Bangalore, her parents tried to be encouraging but realistic. Her mother even gave her extra shopping money, in case she didn't make it. Their only instructions to her were, 'If you don't get through, don't cry.' Pratibha made her way across India, determined and nervous. She wasn't sure if she had prepared enough for whatever came next. But the officer in charge had a very different perspective. 'If you are born to be a naval officer, no one can stop you,' he told the group. 'It isn't something you can study for at the last minute. It is an attitude.'

Pratibha was selected and found herself in a new life. After her initial training in Kochi, Pratibha underwent additional training to become an Air Traffic Controller. Air Traffic Controllers in the Navy control naval fighter aircraft, maritime reconnaissance aircraft and multi-role helicopters both onshore and at sea. It is an important and fulfilling role, but a desk job. Like Vartika, Pratibha was looking for more from her Navy career.

Pratibha started sailing in 2012. Soon after she learnt how to sail, she began taking part in sailing competitions that lasted for 2–3 hours. She loved them, and often excelled, but soon, they felt tame and almost predictable. Pratibha was looking for her next big challenge.

That challenge was just around the corner. The Navy had a larger, deeper plan, but at that point Vartika and Pratibha didn't even have a sense of it. With each call, they volunteered. And with each journey, they felt more confident and comfortable as sailors. They say the lure of the sea is such that once you have been out on it, you keep going back. For Pratibha and Vartika, it was clear – they had found their natural habitat.

Crew Feature: *Lt. Cdr. P Swati*

P Swati grew up in Vizag, not particularly fond either of swimming or the water. But her introduction to the Indian Navy was very close and personal – her mother was a civilian swimming coach to the Indian Navy. Swati was the youngest of three sisters and her parents expected all the girls to be actively engaged in sports and activities. One thing that her father felt strongly about, though, was that one of them should join the armed services. Both Swati's parents believed that serving the country through the defence forces was a privilege and a calling.

For a while, Swati wanted to be a doctor. She even started Class 11 by signing up for biology classes. But along the way, her ambitions took a different direction. She began to understand her father's emotions, and at the same time, her mother's work with the Navy started to take on a deeper significance. Swati applied to and was selected for the Indian Navy, an achievement that filled her whole family with the deepest pride.

After her training, Swati joined the Navy as an Air Traffic Controller. Again, it was a desk job, posted on a base. Like the others, Swati had dreamed of spending her time out at sea. She knew there was more that she could experience from her career, and very soon she found a way!

The Navika Sagar Parikrama

The Navy was planning to put together an all-women crew for a circumnavigation of the world, but before that, they wanted to test the crews' readiness through a series of drills. Each drill was a resounding success, and with each voyage, the Navy was able to identify core members of the new crew. The Navy was convinced, and now a new signal went out.

This was it. Pratibha, Vartika and Swati jumped at the chance to volunteer. It felt like the obvious next step for them. But not everyone was as excited – their families definitely didn't see things the same way. Vartika's parents had never even seen the sea, and now their daughter was setting off on a journey that was certainly going to be arduous, and quite possibly very dangerous. Vartika even invited them to join her on a short boat journey in Mauritius, hoping they would understand the call of the vast unknown. Her mother remained unconvinced, but Vartika, like the others, could hardly wait.

Over the course of the next few months, the six-person crew was selected – first Lt. Cdr. Vartika Joshi, Lt. Cdr. Pratibha Jamwal and

Lt. Cdr. Swati P; then Lieutenants S Vijaya Devi and Payal Gupta; and finally Lt Aishwarya Boddapati.

Crew Feature: Lt Vijayadevi

Shougrakpam Vijaya is one of five children, and the only girl. She was born in Tera Khongshangbi Santhong Sabal in Bishnupur district of landlocked Manipur. Her father Sh. Kunjakeshore Singh was an Army veteran and had served in the Manipur Rifles and her mother, Sh. Binasakhi Devi had been a schoolteacher. Growing up with four brothers, Shou Vijaya couldn't help becoming a tomboy. She ran and climbed and jumped with the best of them. Midway through her childhood, the family moved to Imphal for the children's education. Initially reluctant to let their only daughter move too far away for her education, Shou Vijaya's parents relented, and she first graduated from Dhanamanjuri College of Arts in Manipur, before moving to Delhi to get her Masters in English Literature from Delhi University. And that was when her life changed.

Growing up, Vijaya had always aspired to a career in the Army – it was what she had seen in her family and community, and the thought of being part of a larger mission thrilled her. It was only many years later, when the Navy came to her college for recruiting, that Vijaya was struck with the opportunity of joining the Navy. She was recruited into the Navy, and like the others, went through a rigorous training process before joining her desk job. It had been a long journey from Manipur, but for Vijaya, the journey was far from done. She very quickly realized that she wanted the complete Navy experience, and so she learned how to sail. In 2015, she first cast off her sailing boat in the open waters, when she took part in the Navy Open Sailing Championship held at Indian Naval Academy, Ezhimala. It wasn't smooth sailing in any sense – Vijaya was terrified of capsizing in the ocean. In fact, she

capsized multiple times during the four-day championship, but she was determined to see it through. Every time she capsized her vessel, she got right up and went on. Vijaya won that championship. She won Rs 20,000 and the title of Woman of Steel. But more importantly, the experience cemented her love for adventure out at sea. She was hooked. Even then, though she thought of sailing as fun and adventure, she never even contemplated an enormous, life-changing voyage like the Navika Sagar Parikrama.

Crew Feature: *Lt Payal Gupta*

Payal grew up in Dehradun and spent her childhood watching Indian Military Cadets wearing their crisp uniforms and marching smartly. Even though no one in her family was in the Army, it felt to her like everyone else in Dehradun was, and so it seemed like an obvious career choice. Payal's most cherished dream was to represent India and march in the Republic Day Parade. Then, she felt, she would have achieved her ambition.

She prepared as well as she could and in college, she joined the NCC to be better trained. But after five unsuccessful attempts to pass the Army Short Service Board exams (SSBs), she was forced to revisit her aspiration. Payal was deeply disappointed. She knew that she was meant for a life in the services, but maybe, she decided, it was not going to be in the Army. Payal moved to Gurgaon and started a conventional corporate job with a multinational company. Things were going well, and she was progressing at work. But she hadn't lost hope, or sight of her ultimate goal. In 2012, she heard about the naval recruitment and it struck her that this might be the opportunity for her.

Payal applied and was selected, and in the process, her dream became real. She actually marched in the Republic Day Parade that year. Payal was thrilled – it felt like the achievement of a lifetime.

But after a few months, she realized that it was not enough to just be in the Navy. As an Education Officer, Payal's was largely a desk job, still in Delhi. She felt frustrated and like nothing had really changed in her life after all. In her mind, the Navy signified oceans and sailing and adventure, and, at her desk, she didn't have a sense of any of those. Payal was determined to learn how to sail. She was determined to do something bigger. When the signal went out for an all-woman crew, she literally jumped out of her seat. She was ready.

Crew Feature: Lt Aishwarya Boddapati

Aishwarya Boddapati's father was in the CISF (Central Industrial Security Force), and she first saw the sea when she was three, and the family was posted in Vizag. It terrified her, and she refused to go anywhere near it.

A few years later, the family moved to Hyderabad, and Aishwarya spent the rest of her school years there. Her family travelled constantly, taking in the sights, smells and cultures of new places in India, and Aishwarya developed a deep wanderlust. She knew that when she grew up, she wanted to travel the world and have as many new experiences as possible.

When Aishwarya completed her schooling, she decided to follow her passion and chose to study metallurgy engineering. Aishwarya loved college – she was studying something she felt passionate about, and she had a broad circle of friends. But after college, things got unexpectedly difficult. Jobs in metallurgy engineering were only in steel plants or automotive industry factories, and although she applied for job after job, the companies only wanted male candidates. It was during an internship at the DRDO lab that her father spotted an ad in the paper. The Navy was looking for technical officers. It listed criteria for age and qualifications. But no gender criteria.

Aishwarya hadn't actively thought about the services as a career option, but at the same time, somewhere inside she had always wanted a job with a uniform, just like her dad. She applied, was called for assessment, and very quickly got selected. Both her parents, but especially her father, encouraged Aishwarya to join. Not everyone gets a chance to join the services, they said. Joining the Indian Navy was enormously prestigious, a great opportunity, and Aishwarya jumped at it.

She joined up, and was soon sent to training. Despite the intensely challenging physical requirements, Aishwarya loved that time in her life. Batchmates from training went on to become her closest friends, and one of them, Pratibha Jamwal, went on to become much more. After the first session of training, Aishwarya was sent to IIT Delhi for her technical training, where she also met Vartika Joshi, one year her senior. It was also while at Delhi that Aishwarya discovered DAPSA (the Directorate of Adventure Physical Fitness and Sports Activities) and her world opened up. DAPSA was responsible for organizing different adventure activities—mountaineering, paragliding, river rafting—and Aishwarya threw herself wholeheartedly into all of them. She couldn't believe her luck in being able to do so many exciting things, through the Navy.

During her first posting in Port Blair, Aishwarya first met Cdr. Donde and Pratibha and Vartika aboard *Mhadhei*. A few months later, when the signal went out for women volunteers for a new voyage (what would ultimately become the Navika Sagar Parikrama), Aishwarya volunteered. She didn't tell her parents, though – she knew that they had started looking for a groom for her and this probably wouldn't sound like either a good idea or good timing to them.

She got her appointment letter only six months later. Now Aishwarya had a task ahead of her. She had to convince her boss—which would be hard—and her parents, which was even harder. She finally bought time with her parents, saying that she would try it out as a volunteer for a few months, and if it wasn't a fit, she could step out at any time. They were unconvinced, but Aishwarya went ahead. The first time she was going to sail on the open sea to Mauritius on *Mhadei*, Aishwarya asked her parents to join her in Goa and see the boat. By the end of the day, her father was so excited by the experience, he almost wanted to go sailing with her! All her life, Aishwarya's parents had been her biggest role models, especially her father. He was a man of great integrity, and Aishwarya had seen him treat all the women in his life equally and respectfully. When in doubt, his principles were always the ones she deferred to, so her parents' approval gave Aishwarya a new burst of motivation. She was ready to go.

The crew all came from different places and different cadres. But there was one thing they shared – an itch for adventure.

The Men Behind the Women

Vice Admiral Manohar Prahlad Awati, popularly known as the Father of Indian Circumnavigation Adventures, conceptualized a series of voyages designed to showcase the Indian Navy's skills and prowess. The Sagar Parikrama project was launched in 2007, planning solo circumnavigations on Indian-built vessels. This led to the construction of the INSV *Mhadei* and INSV *Tarini*. In 2010, Cdr. Dilip Donde became the first Indian to record a solo circumnavigation. He was followed soon after by Cdr. Abhilash Tomy, who became the first Indian and only the second Asian to do a non-stop solo circumnavigation. With those two massive achievements under their belt, Vice Admiral Awati naturally began to think about the next big step. Clearly, it was

Vice Admiral Manohar Awati with Lt Cdr Vartika Joshi and Lt Aishwarya Boddapati

time to showcase the role of women in the Navy. There was one, very significant challenge though – no women in the Indian Navy had any relevant sailing experience. On top of that, circumnavigation called for much more than just a knowledge of sailing – it required deep knowledge of ship running, maintenance, naval communications and a number of other technical skills that could literally mean the difference between life and death out at sea. He, Cdr. Donde and Cdr. Tomy brainstormed a little, and out of that brainstorming was born the Navika Sagar Parikrama (circumnavigation of the globe by Women Seafarers). By sailing on an Indian designed-and-built vessel, INSV *Tarini*, and harnessing environment-friendly renewable energy, the voyage aimed to make a statement in many ways.

Commander Dilip Donde graduated from the Indian National Defence Academy and was commissioned in the Indian Navy on 1 January 1990. He specialized as a Clearance Diver and held various command,

Commander Dilip Dhonde

staff and instructional appointments before volunteering to undertake a solo unassisted circumnavigation with only the assistance of the wind, and no engine power. He succeeded. He covered over 23,000 nautical miles and spent 270 days alone at sea, often in treacherous conditions. With this achievement, Cdr. Dhonde joined an elite group of solo circumnavigators. He was awarded the Shaurya Chakra, the peacetime equivalent of the Vir Chakra award.

Captain Atool Sinha is an Asian Games Silver Medallist and was Officer-in-charge of Ocean Sailing Node at the time of the crew's training. A skilled sailor himself, he trained the crew not just on the technical aspects of ocean sailing, but more importantly, on the mental preparedness needed to survive an expedition of this nature. He continued to be their mentor and guide them through the nine months voyage that followed.

The Journey

This was the team that conceived of and pushed to get approval for the Navika Sagar Parikrama. At the same time, the team was aware that this would be an enormous ask – the training would be exhausting and the journey, over several months, would be both intense and dangerous. The crew would have to be away from their families for almost a year, and work nearly non-stop in shifts to keep their vessel in working condition. The men decided that the only option would be to ask for volunteers, rather than select from existing candidates. They also started by having women join mixed-gender crews for shorter voyages, so that they would get a true sense of life at sea. Cdr. Donde, who had volunteered to train the crew, was clear – he didn't want anyone to have romantic notions of going out to sea and enjoying the sunset. Given that no woman in the

Navy had the relevant technical skills, all he was looking for was hard work and a willingness to learn. More importantly, the crew had to have the strength of mind and personality to be self-sufficient. Out at sea, there was no one to fall back on.

> *'The only way to cope is preparing and anticipating',*
>
> **Vartika Joshi**

The women had a long journey before they could set off on their newly-commissioned Navy vessel, INSV *Tarini*.

For almost three years, the crew trained in Mumbai at the Indian Naval Watermanship Training Centre (INWTC), and at various schools in the southern Naval base in Kochi. There were classes on theory, engineering, mapping and navigation and ship maintenance. Once out at sea, they would have no one to rely on. They would have to anticipate the unanticipatable. And the only way to do that would be hard work and lots and lots of drills.

They worked most closely during this time with Cdr. Donde and Capt. Atool Sinha.

The training was intentionally intense. At sea, your strongest ally is your boat. If the boat survives, you survive. Cdr. Donde knew this, and he wanted the crew to understand it as well. He wanted them to be able to care for their vessel completely, and independently. Apart from the many theory classes, the women spent hours and hours and hours, sleeves rolled up, learning about boat cleaning, repairing and maintenance. He made it clear to the team that he would consider them ready when they could take the boat for a sortie (short journey or trip) independently.

Oct 27th 2015

Oct 27 saw the first overnight sortie of the Trinity onboard Mhadei. Plan was to cast off around 1230 hrs and get back to Mandovi next morning around 10 AM. The team managed to finish all admin works and arrange for food, water and other supplies in time. By 1245 hrs we were out at sea. We decided to head west for a few miles before opening to South and continue with it through the night. We were expecting 4-7 kn of S-SW winds during the day veering to N-NE by the night. Sailed in pretty light winds in a broad reach making a Southerly headway but the headway seemed sluggish, hence took a call to put up the only Genneker that we are left with at the moment, the A3 Genneker. Our mentor says that the day he doesn't have to come out to help us with sailing the boat and he can peacefully sit on his bunk and read his books for three consecutive days, he would know that we are ready. Well, he did get his book this time and we also tried our best to not disturb him with the boat's activities. Fortunately, he didn't come out very often except once or twice when he might have lost his resistance. Hopefully next time we sail, he regains his lost resistance!

'Gender cannot stop you from going around the world,' Cdr. Donde once memorably told them. 'The sea is gender neutral.' As far as he was concerned, they were sailors in the making and it was his job to prepare them for the job ahead.

Along the way, though, there was resistance and skepticism from many other sources. One person famously asked the crew, 'What happens if one of you gets married? Won't you drop out then?'

The women retorted, 'Would you ask the same question of a man? What has marriage got to do with this voyage?' And they carried on training!

In 2016 they sailed on INSV *Mhadei* to Mauritius and back, their first voyage as a crew. Since none of them had prior sailing experience, it was not clear who should captain the crew. The Captain of the crew needs to be the first amongst equals – while everyone has to have the same knowledge and abilities, the choice of Captain, especially for a voyage like this, was important. At sea, and in a crisis, the Captain would ask for all opinions, but the final decision had to be hers; and her authority had to be strong. To start with, the crew followed an interesting practice, Skipper for the Day. They took turns captaining the vessel every time they went out for a trial run and seeing what it felt like to make decisions for the team.

In February 2016, after much discussion and negotiation with the Naval Board, the crew was given approval to set off on their first voyage without their coach. The night before they set sail, the crew received word that Vartika Joshi was the Skipper for their first independent voyage.

The voyage was extremely successful, and they followed it up in May with a longer one from Goa to Cape Town. The crew was growing in confidence, and it was now clear that Vartika would be the best Captain for the circumnavigation. Pratibha was her second in command. And as a team, the entire crew complemented each other's skill sets.

Over the course of the next few years, as a crew, they completed a stunning 20,000 nautical miles in shorter journeys. It wasn't easy. Apart from the hard physical work, they were also preparing themselves mentally to be away from home.

Today marks our 31st·day at sea. People feel that one day here is no different from other but a day at sea is always different and we consider ourselves more of amphibians now (no wonder jammy [Lt Cdr Pratibha] and aish [Lt Aishwarya] call themselves croc and gator). As we have been away for a month now let us tell you about what we miss the most about being on the land and how it feels to spend so long at sea.

Starting what we miss about the land the first thing that comes to our mind is some quality time with family and friends. It's been a month and we have been in touch with them only virtually and can communicate by an email or two in a day. We missed some important occasions too - birthdays, anniversaries and the farewell of our mentor. So all of us are looking forward to getting back and making up for the lost time.

At the same time, the many weeks spent together created the strongest friendships and bonds. This was to save their lives one day, but they didn't know it yet.

They got to know each other deeply, sharing their ambitions, dreams and hopes with each other.

And they always found time to joke around a little bit, including poking fun at their mentors.

The crew with Cdr Dhonde

Day 38-Art or Sailing?
We had some neighbours going past us for a while like a flock of albatross which are quite a sight for any observant birdwatcher. They sit on the surface of the sea when the swell is quite high like ducks (probably even take a nap) while taking rest, and when they take flight they hardly ever flap their wings even while flying against the strongest of winds. It's as if they are giving us a message - when facing difficulties in life, sit over it and think and when you face it, do it without fluttering.
The next set of neighbours were a school of dolphins. Usually the dolphins, which are our frequent visitors, outnumber and overtake us every time they visit. This time around they outnumbered us by thousands, visible over a range of 2 miles. They were in no hurry, and overtook us splashing, singing and flipping on the sea, busy in their gymnastics. They came quite close to Mhadei as if welcoming her into African waters.

We also witnessed a full moon night at sea which got us all philosophical, dreamy and poetic.
….

In our last post readers could witness some fine poetry by our amateur poet shou which got us to discussing what fine arts we wanted to pursue when we were young VJ philosophically says she always thought she would become a poet. People who know her can agree to it, as her mother has written some lovely poems for Mhadei which we will publish one of these days

Jammy thought she was quite the singer of her era when she was a kid; her selection and choice of music indicate the making of a singer

Aish however thinks she could have made a good standup comedian as she bores everyone on the boat with her ant and elephant jokes and also reads out loud some jokes mailed by her father (if only she could control her own laughter while narrating these jokes)!

Shou is being asked to seriously consider her movie-making skills. She even gave quite a demonstration of her directorial skills when she directed VJ and Aish to take up a reef of mainsail with great finesse.

Swatcat is thinking of becoming an interior decorator, a good example of it can be her own house which she has done up with expertise

Our Dancing queen Puko probably thinks of dancing even while sleeping, given the fact that she is quite a show stopper on the dance floor. She even stops people from dancing to show her puko moves Yeah! ..

Whether it is art or science, what we wanted to become as compared to what we have become is a different ball game altogether. We became ocean sailors in pursuit of action and adventure…

And it has led us here where we belong and the best thing about it is it doesn't stop us from pursuing our skills as a poet singer or writer; neither will it stop us from going across boundaries and becoming more seasoned by each passing day.

Every day is a new lesson and every voyage is a new chapter of experience.

Signing off while gearing up for new lessons and sailing away across the next boundary.

Crew Feature: INSV Tarini

In 2017, INSV *Tarini* was ready for trials and successfully completed trial voyages to Mumbai, Porbandar and Mauritius.

INSV *Tarini*, along with her older sister INSV *Mhadei*, were conceived of, designed and built as indigenous naval vessels. In other words, they were completely made in India. *Tarini* was born (constructed) at the Aquarius Shipyard in Divar, Goa. Measuring 17 metres in length, her hull is built of wood-coe and fibreglass sandwich. Her mast was custom-built by Southern Spars and is 25 metres tall. *Tarini* was named after the Tara Tarini temple. After completing a number of sea trials, she was handed over to the Indian Navy on 16 February 2017. Like her team members, *Tarini* was ready to sail, and raring for adventures on the high seas.

Now the entire crew—six officers and *Tarini*—was ready. Or as ready as they ever could be.

The evening before the launch, Vartika should have been jittery with excitement and nerves. As their skipper, it was up to her to bring everyone back home. She felt the weight of her responsibility and the weight of the voyage. The next day, they were going to be seen off by the Chief Minister of Goa, the Indian Navy Chief and India's Defence Minister. It was momentous. And terrifying. But, as is often the case before an important event, she was focused on just being prepared. The whole crew was the same. There was no time for nervousness or fear. As a team, they had to get *Tarini* ready to cast off. And they had all of their own preparations – food, water, clothes. Their families had all come to help them load. All of the mental preparation for this voyage had happened over the three years leading up to this; now the crew was ready to set off on their adventures. The only thing Vartika was thinking about was casting off properly the next day. She believed that a good start makes all the difference to a voyage.

Leg 1: Goa to Fremantle, Australia

As the crew set sail, they had mixed emotions. They were going to be away for almost a year. During this time, they would be missing more milestones, birthdays and anniversaries. They were leaving behind husbands, parents (Captain Vartika's mother was unwell and would be going through surgery while she was at sea) and friends. To get through, they would have to draw into every reserve of strength, willpower and teamwork. They would have no one but themselves to rely on.

At the same time, if they achieved what they were setting out to do, it would literally be trailblazing.

They would be opening new avenues for women not just in India, and not just in the services. They would be showcasing what grit, determination and training can do. And they would go down in history.

They were being watched by an entire nation.

September 15th
Today is the sixth day of our voyage. This night while I was on the middle watch, a cargo vessel named Gulf Moon on our starboard bow was approaching close to us, hence I quickly called it on the VHF set and he immediately agreed to alter his course and keep clear of us. At sea, I have learnt that seafarers are very nice and polite and responsive, unlike on land, where we find people arguing for no reasons in the middle of a traffic and refuse to give way. These little things at sea teach us to respect humanity. After Gulf Moon altered the course, he called us back and in an inquisitive voice he said 'Ma'am, are you the same sailing vessel which is circumnavigating the globe, as I read about it on FB'. When VJ affirmed it, saying that we had started our voyage on 10 Sep, Gulf Moon wished us a safe and happy sailing. Honestly, in the middle of the night, it felt like a friend calling us to say hello, which also made us overcome a tough long night amongst the fishing traffic.
We also saw many fishing boats in the last few days, one of them looked like a party boat as the fishermen joyfully recovered their nets, dancing in unison on the tunes of ' Ullu ka Pattha Hai!'. Needless to say, we didn't miss the opportunity to dance back from our little boat and it almost became a DJ moment!
September 18th
It's been exactly a week that we set sail from Goa and finally the day has come when we cross the Indian peninsula. We will come back now only next year... Nostalgic...this longing and sense of separation from motherland is quite overwhelming; probably one of the reasons why we were hugging the coastline all the way down...

Nayi Umang,
Navy Adventure!

Ensures smooth sailing!

The first leg of the trip was on the Indian Ocean, seas that were both calm and familiar territory. The crew felt extremely comfortable, and quickly settled into routines of four-hour shifts, cooking duty, rest-time, boat maintenance and, most importantly, time to just relax and enjoy the sea.

They also found unusual solutions for some daily domestic issues. *Tarini* was a small boat, and a somewhat tight fit for six people. The cooking stove was fixed to the wall, but as the boat rocked around, so did the cook. So, in stormy weather, whoever was on cooking duty tethered themselves! There were also a few basic appliances, but no washing machine. After a few different ideas, the crew struck upon a novel way to do their laundry. They would tie their clothes together, put them on a long tether and let them trail behind *Tarini* in the water. Occasionally, they lost the odd sock or shorts, but in general it turned out to be an efficient system, and saved them one tedious housekeeping chore. And so, the first few weeks passed. Along the way, there were minor adventures.

Life is a stepwise adventure. Sometimes, the more we explore, the more it leaves us bewildered with its mysteries. Yesterday was one such night. The first watch (Swatcat & Gator) sighted a blob of light at a distance right astern of us. It looked like a fishing vessel initially, that being an obvious interpretation considering our experiences with the fishermen in the past few days; nor would it display in our automatic identification system. As they constantly kept a watch on the light they realised the bearing of the light with respect to us wouldn't change at all. Considering a speed of 8 km that we were constantly making, it felt like quite a speed for a fishing vessel motoring in choppy weather. After about an hour of constant following by this light it started closing us at a greater speed and as it drew nearer it strangely never made the slightest of noise a motoring boat would normally make. It closed us, and then it moved back to its previous bearing right astern of us. For the next one hour we were constantly being chased by this; what we named a USO (Unidentified Sailing Object). As I woke up, Swatcat and Gator made me privy to this strange thing they had sighted. As we kept observing, our suspicion would only increase. This little light wouldn't cease to chase us... We thereafter switched off all internal lights, even our navigation lights, and altered course to check if it would still follow us. To our pleasant surprise, the light gradually faded away after that. Mystery prevails and maybe we won't ever come to know what this strange little thing was!

Soon the night amazed us yet another time. The waters shone with many many dolphins swooping past us, visible only as streaks of bioluminescence criss-crossing in the vicinity of the boat. It's something we could never capture in our cams (cameras); only the eyes can absorb the eternal beauty of this entire universe that's perennially active under us.

Unfortunately, soon after entering the first leg, they found themselves well and truly in the Doldrums. The Doldrums are a belt around the Equator known for their calm winds and seas. In theory, this sounds lovely and peaceful, but for the crew this was both extremely frustrating—*Tarini* needed winds to propel herself forward—and potentially dangerous. There is no shortage of naval stories of sailboats stuck in the Doldrums, unable to move and slowly running out of supplies. Without winds, they were just bobbing along in the water, inching towards the Equator, but without much momentum.

And then, the RO (Reverse Osmosis) water filtration system on the boat broke down. The crew took turns being mechanics, and attempting to fix it, or at least to understand the issue. Despite much tinkering around, they were unable to figure out how to get it working again. Several thousands of miles away from the nearest landmass, they now had a very real and immediate problem. At sea, with the high salt content and dehydration levels, the crew would not last longer than a week without drinking water. There was no choice but to break into their stores of water bottles. Swati took charge of counting and rationing drinking water. They were allowed 1.5 litres per day. For everything non-essential, they had to make do, or do without.

'Water, water everywhere, but not a drop to drink.' The crew was reminded of 'The Rime of the Ancient Mariner', a poem written in 1798, telling the story of a sailor stuck in still oceans, with only access to salt water. It was stunning to realize that out at sea, their dangers were the same fundamental dangers that sailors had been facing for centuries.

Crossing the Equator

Crossing the Equator might no longer seem like a big deal to any of us these days – we do it easily and often when we take a flight, for example. Modern Naval vessels cross the Equator constantly. But crossing the Equator for the first time is still a time-honoured tradition. New sailors were often known as Pollywags until they had crossed for the first time. After the Initiation Ceremony, sailors were called Shellbacks, meaning that King Neptune had accepted them as one of his trusted shellbacks (an experienced sailor).

Slowly, painfully, they crossed the Equator and achieved their first big milestone. In spite of severe rationing, they celebrated with a cake baked by Swati and lots of loud, off-key singing.

The moment they crossed the Equator, things started looking up. The winds gathered speed, *Tarini* started racing forwards to Fremantle, and then, gloriously, it started to rain.

After weeks and weeks of heat and humidity, it was wonderful to see the skies open up. The women danced on the deck, showered on the deck, even washed their hair on the deck. They felt squeaky clean after a long time. They also had a brainwave – rainwater harvesting. They opened out the sails to act as collection pools, drained out the water into buckets for storage, and in the process, gathered enough water for the rest of the leg to Australia. It felt very empowering to harness nature for all their needs.

A few days later, *Tarini* eased her way into Fremantle, Australia, and the crew disembarked for a few days. The first, eventful leg had been completed.

Leg 2: Fremantle to Lyttleton, New Zealand

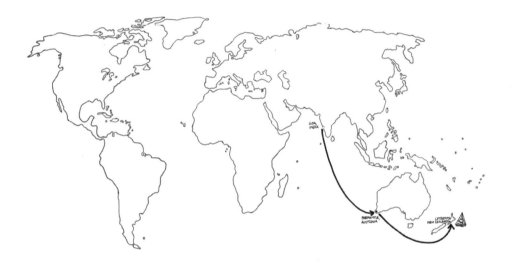

After a few days of repair and rest for everyone, and lots of good food from the Indian families of Australia, *Tarini* set off again. The crew was relaxed and well-fed and filled with the warmth of all the encounters they had had. Meeting all the Indian host-families had filled many of them with a strong sense of longing and homesickness. They had successfully completed the first leg of their journey. At the same time, they knew that from now onwards they would be leaving the familiar comforts of the Indian Ocean. And now there was no turning back – they were sailing deeper into their voyage and further away from home.

Soon, though, they got back into their on-board routines, and started enjoying the wonderful and often unexpected experiences that every day threw at them.

It is always a surprise when nature catches you unaware just when you are lost into its mesmerising beauty. Such was our awe when we witnessed AURORAS - the southern lights.. Mind you, only a lucky few get to witness this at sea. Let me share some wonders of nature we witnessed on our way to Lyttelton, New Zealand, our second pit stop, and some wonderful moments we had over there. We were fortunate to have witnessed auroras three consecutive nights on our way to Lyttelton. They were these green streak of lights strewn across the sky glowing dark somewhere and not so bright elsewhere. We were smitten watching them, and even tried to capture them, but I guess we need special lenses for that. No wonder people plan a trip to Iceland to witness the northern lights. Some wonders of nature can only be experienced. It is supposed to happen because of the high magnetic forces that exist at the poles and at that time, we were at the southernmost tip of leg 2, just about to climb our way up to Lyttelton. When we were climbing our way up and were quite close to the shore, hugging the coast to gain some speed one pleasant morning, we saw some dolphins from far closing in on us. Upon closer examination, we discovered that they were quite huge in size and fins located closer to the tail. They were so huge that their proximity to the boat got us worried, but smart mammals that they are, one wandering dolphin dived below the boat and surfaced on the other side as we watched it dumbstruck. A little research on the internet a while later told us that these were pilot whales, which are a kind of dolphin found usually in the region this part of the year. I feel like Alice in Wonderland, narrating all the wonders I get to witness here…

Leg 3: Lyttleton to Falkland Islands

As the crew left New Zealand, they were a little nervous. They were now sailing into the somewhat treacherous waters of the South Pacific Sea. The next landmass, help and humanity would be many, many thousands of miles away, and they sensed this could be the toughest leg of their journey. It had gotten quite cold, and somewhere, they knew, there was a storm brewing. The Pacific passage of the voyage would be approximately 5500 nautical miles – the longest leg in their journey. They would now experience windchill, sub-zero temperatures and a shift in wind patterns. They needed to be prepared for literally anything.

Soon after setting off, there was a snapping noise and they realized one of *Tarini*'s sails had come loose. It would need to be tethered back, especially given what they expected in the coming weeks. The only problem was that fixing the sail would mean climbing all the way to the top – a height of 25 metres (approximately eight apartment floors up). Even in the currently calm waters, it was a dangerous thing to

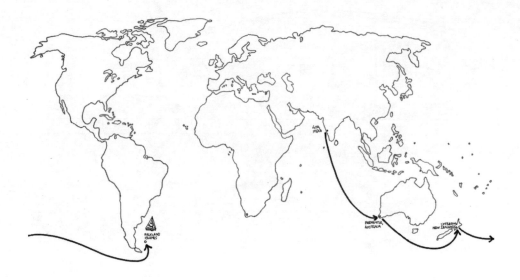

do. Falling from that height into the sea below almost certainly meant disappearing into the water. But it was a job that urgently needed to be done, and as both Skipper and the most experienced sailor on board, Vartika stepped forward. She waited for the sea to get as calm as possible, thinking about her strategy to get up and stay up. Her tether was her lifeline. Slowly, supported by shouts of encouragement from the rest of the crew, Vartika inched up the sails, Spiderwoman-style. Once at the top, it took her a long time to fix the swinging sails, working with one arm and clinging on with the other. Finally, it was done, and she inched her way back down. She had been up there for only an hour, but it had felt like a lifetime, and as the others rushed to help her down, she was exhausted.

The sails were now fixed, and the crew could relax for a while. But there was a sense of what was brewing. They say that sailors can sense a storm in their bones, and this crew definitely could. Slowly but surely, the winds started picking up speed and intensity, moving from 30 knots to 45 knots. The crew knew they could not change course too much – it would make them lose time on their voyage. So, even as they monitored the storm, they kept moving forward. They got to work

preparing *Tarini* for battle. They needed to protect their vessel and keep her safe. If either the boat or any of the crew were impacted, the entire expedition would be at stake. Everything that could be battened down or tethered, was.

One day before the storm, they experienced first hail and then snow. It was stunning – literally the first time any of them had seen snow at sea. But it also meant that they couldn't let down their guard for even a minute. After the hailstorm, they had to keep adjusting the sails to stay on track.

Soon after, they saw what they had been anticipating on the horizon. It looked like a massive storm, and their tiny vessel was sailing right into the heart of it. Vartika had an idea. They set course for a direction opposite to that of the storm. If they moved fast enough, they hoped, they would just be able to scoot past it.

But the storm was wilier than they had expected. In an unexpected move, the tail winds of the storm grabbed hold of *Tarini* and pulled her and her crew right back into its path. There was no escape – *Tarini* was now well and clearly in the middle of the perfect storm, and the crew now had to fight the hardest they had ever fought to keep their boat together.

For about three days, they stood on guard, with the wind speeds constantly picking up. Then on 8 January 2018, it became clear that things were only going to get rougher. Wind speeds were now often at 60 knots (over a 100km per hour) and higher; they had lost network, contact with land was patchy at best, and anyway, there was nothing that anyone from land could do to help them at this point. The crew and *Tarini* would have to ride it out.

The waves at that point were often 10–12 metres high (as tall as a three-storey building) and there were mountains of water coming up from behind them. So tall sometimes that they couldn't see the sky above. And so loud, they couldn't hear each other speak.

Swati, Payal and Aishwarya stayed down below the decks; Vijaya and Pratibha were out on the deck; and as Skipper, Vartika stood at the steering wheel. More than anyone, it was her job to hold *Tarini* steady and keep her safe. They were all soaked through, tethered to the boat and exhausted from three nights of no sleep. Vartika shouted at them to take their base positions. And that was when the big wave hit them. Outside, the three women watched in horror as the massive wave, more than eight meters high, engulfed them.

Inside the cabin, Aishwarya braced, and then felt the enormous wave slam *Tarini*. The boat rocked completely from side to side. Payal went flying across the room, hitting her head on a board and blacking out. As soon as they were able to, the other two rushed to help revive her. Then Aishwarya looked out and onto the deck. She could see Pratibha and Vijaya on the deck, crawling towards the steering wheel, where Vartika should have been. She looked at the steering wheel but could see no one there!

'Where's Vartika ma'am? Where's Vartika?' she shouted in shock. For a terrifying split second, the crew couldn't spot their Captain. And then they saw her. The water had thrown her across onto the other side of the deck. She was lying there, bruised, but gripping the steering wheel. She was safe.

Later, Vartika told them that when the wave hit them, for a few moments she was inside the water. She let go of the wheel, allowing the boat to swing with the wind and follow the wave. For those few seconds, she flailed about, unable to feel anything solid beneath her or in front of her, and she wondered if she had been swept off board. Fortunately, seconds later, she grasped the steering wheel again, and realized the tether had saved her life.

The enormous wave passed, but the crew was drenched and freezing. Water had even gone into their living space, so many of their supplies were wet, and all their spare clothes too. The battle continued for nineteen hours. It took two, sometimes three crew members at a time to manage the wheel and keep *Tarini* steady. They were exhausted,

but had to keep doing two-hour shifts. It was now night and so dark that they couldn't even see what lay ahead. The crew steered with the help of the sound of the waves – the waves needed to be coming from behind them, not the side. It was terrifying, but also incredible as they came together. They didn't need to speak to each other to know what to do or where to be. Their years of training kicked in and they moved together wordlessly.

Finally, they were through the worst of it, and when morning came, *Tarini* saw sunshine for the first time in three days. That morning dawned peaceful and sunny, and they felt like the skies had cleared. The crew of *Tarini* were all on the deck to watch the sunrise. Like their vessel, they were battered, but they had survived.

Every sailor has his (or in this case, her) story of the Perfect Storm. This is the storm to end all the storms. The storm that shows just how powerful the sea can be. The storm that can be fatal. For the crew of *Tarini*, this was that Perfect Storm.

After the storm, they made relatively smooth progress towards the Falkland Islands. The storm had damaged their engine. An engine is usually not required for circumnavigation sailing, but very often it's needed to guide the vessel into the port. Luckily, in this case, even without the engine, the winds came to their rescue, and led *Tarini* to port. There was a crowd of people waiting to meet the exhausted heroines.

Leg 4 : Falklands to Cape Town

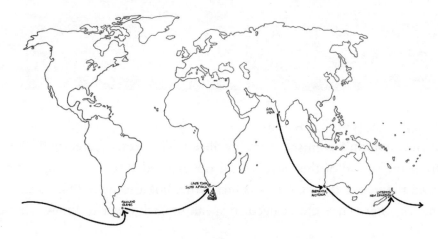

The journey from Falklands to Cape Town was predictable and relatively peaceful. *Tarini* hummed along, and the crew settled into a comfortable routine. Along the way, they celebrated some birthdays and milestones, and when they docked at Cape Town, they were in for a lovely surprise. The Indian community had gathered there to greet them with Holi colours. The crew was especially excited as it was the first (and only) festival they had been able to celebrate on land during the journey. As always, the time on land was both relaxing and full of social engagements.

Leg 5: Cape Town to Goa

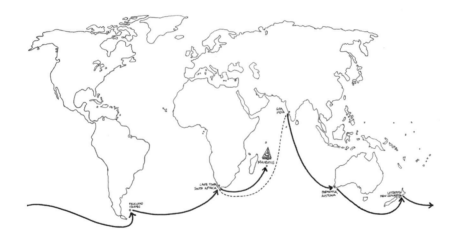

Finally, they set off from Cape Town, towards Goa. Once again, they were sailing in familiar waters and they were all eagerly looking forward to getting back home.

Things were going smoothly (as they always do, just before an incident!) when the crew heard a loud snapping sound. Rushing up to the deck, they saw the steering wheel spinning loosely, without any tethers. Somehow the wires had broken and the steering wheel was no longer connected to the rudder. This was rather like driving a car with no steering wheel. Without a way to guide the boat, they were completely at the mercy of the winds. After about eight hours of mechanical work, they came up with a makeshift solution, that of making one steering gear serviceable. But they were entering the cyclone season, and couldn't take a chance on their last leg.

The crew had no choice, but to call in for help. After some consultation at the Navy headquarters, Captain Atool Sinha spoke to them with a solution. *Tarini* could be repaired, he said, but they would need to make an unplanned stop—and extension—at Mauritius, not far away.

Vartika and the rest of the crew were depleted by now. They managed to guide *Tarini* into the port in Mauritius, and here they needed to make a decision. Mauritius was really so close to home. They could tell the Navy that the voyage was largely done, leave *Tarini* to get repaired and fly home, and see their families in a few hours' time. Everyone would understand, and they had practically completed their voyage. But they unanimously agreed not to do this. It felt too much like quitting, and just when they were so close to success. They owed it to Vice Admiral Awati, Cdr. Donde, Capt. Sinha and all the hundreds of other well-wishers and helpers along the way. They also felt very strongly that they had started this mission as a crew of seven and they would complete the mission as a crew of seven. There was no question of leaving *Tarini* behind.

In Mauritius, they were met by a Naval crew who had flown down with supplies and tools, and after a few days *Tarini* was shipshape again.

As they were finally closing in on their last leg, they were met and accompanied by some unexpected underwater troops – a group of whale sharks flanked them. It felt like an early welcome committee.

And finally, there it was! They saw shore – Goa. All six of them stood

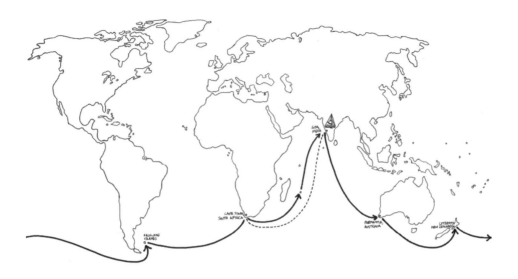

on board, approaching home. They were triumphant but pensive, as it dawned on them that now the adventure was over. After years of training and 254 days of sailing, their voyage was done.

At sea, they had been everything – chefs, nurses, mechanics, sailors and hair stylists. They had met foreign dignitaries, been hosted by warm families across the globe and had told their stories to hundreds of excited schoolchildren. They had seen more rainbows than they could recall, birds that they couldn't identify and been escorted on their journey by dolphins and whale sharks. They had argued, danced, cooked, celebrated birthdays, festivals and milestones. They had supported each other as a team, looked after and been looked after by Tarini. They had faced down their perfect storm and survived. They had enjoyed and been overwhelmed by the vastness of the sea and the sky. And they had drawn on every inner reserve of mental and physical strength to circumnavigate the globe. They were relieved to be back home. But equally, they felt a deep, combined pride at what they had managed to achieve. The six women who returned to Goa were very different from the ones who had left less than a year ago. It felt like nine months, but also like the blink of an eye.

Lt Cdr Vartika Joshi
with Defence Minister Nirmala Sitharaman and Capt Atool Sinha

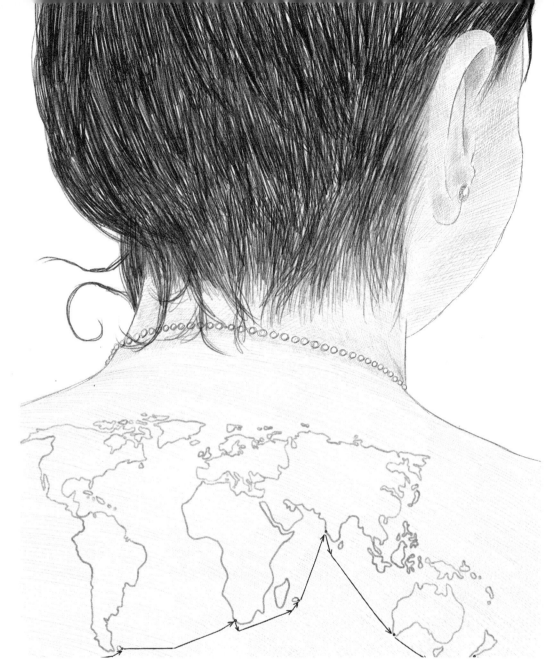

Tarini's journey tattooed on a crew member's back

It was the end of a mission. The end of a goal. The crew felt a sense of achievement, but also mild melancholy. This was all they had worked towards for over three years. They had actually been on two Parikramas

– the first three years of training, and then the actual voyage. In each of their minds, they were wondering – what next?

Vartika and the crew stayed focused, though. Their responsibility was not done until the rope was thrown over and they had safely delivered *Tarini* back to shore.

They knew they would be greeted by the press, and by high-ranking Naval officials, government officials, their mentors, and most importantly, their families. The Indian Naval Fighter Aircraft were doing a fly-past in their honour. But, just for a moment, they wanted to savour the sea, along with their friend, *Tarini*.

From the shore, their mentor, Cdr. Dilip Donde watched as well, savouring their success. For him, the more enjoyable part had been watching them mature and grow as sailors. Captain Vartika had sailed for the first time in 2014. Only Swati had sailed before as an NCC cadet, but as a crew, they had come to him raw. Over three years, the crew had gone from being starry-eyed and inexperienced, to becoming confident in their knowledge and achievements. From never having been at sea before, they were now part of an elite group of circumnavigators across the world. He was thrilled and proud.

There is a sailors' superstition – 'Women at sea are unlucky.' The crew of the Navika Sagar Parikrama believed in no such thing. They made their own luck, worked hard, and did something epic. They literally plotted their own course. And they made history.

Vice Admiral Awati passed away peacefully a few months after the voyage. Cdr. Donde is retired from the Navy, and has written a book, *The First Indian*, chronicling his time at sea.

In 2018, the crew of the Navika Sagar Parikrama were each awarded the Nau Sena Award in recognition of their great gallantry. They continue to serve in the Navy in various capacities. And are always ready for adventure.

In 2020, it was decided that female naval officers can serve on warships, and also be eligible for permanent commission. As of September 2020, Sub Lieutenant Kumudini Tyagi and Sub Lieutenant Riti Singh became the first women to stay and serve on a Naval warship – which paves the way for future frontline duty. There are, at this point, about 500 women in the Indian Navy.

A verse to the sea

To the vast expanse of the deep blue sea
To a world above you and me

To the birds that sing a song to Thee
To the sea I heard that sets one free

To existence enormous you hide underneath
So aloof from this crazy breed

Yet the closest in your reach
Behold, until we meet

For what you seek is what I seek
I am the end, you are the means.

Lt. Cdr. Vartika Joshi

Every day, women in the Armed Forces
are moving the boundaries forward,
each in their own way. And they do so
on the shoulders of the many intrepid
women who served before them.

Maya Chandrasekaran is, in no particular order, an author, traveller, mother, investor, climate warrior and progressive. She lives in Bangalore with her husband and two sons, and is generally located lost in a good book.

Meera Naidu is an artist and textile designer who has settled in Bangalore after growing up all over India. When her son lets her, she works on reimagining traditional craft and design with communities across India. She is a keen scuba diver, lover of golden shoes and chow-chow baath, and now an illustrator.

More books in the Timeless Biographies series

Amrita Sher-Gil: Rebel with a Paintbrush

Anita Vachharajani

Illustrated by Kalyani Ganapathy

An artist? A dreamer? A rebel? Who exactly was Amrita Sher-Gil? She was a little bit of all these things, really. Amrita grew up with a great sense of mischief and adventure in two very different worlds, in a village near Budapest, Hungary, and among the cool, green hills of colonial Simla. She defied headmistresses, teachers, art critics and royalty to make her own determined way in the world of grown-ups and art. Join her on a journey through her life, a journey that takes her family through World Wars and political turmoil as they travel in pursuit of love, a home and a modern, artistic education for Amrita!

She Can You Can:
The A-Z Book of Iconic Indian Women

Garima Kushwaha

Illustrated by Anastasia Damani

An A to Z biography of iconic Indian women, one for each letter of the English alphabet. Each character is represented by an illustrative sketch and a 500-word summary. This inspirational and motivational book includes the achievements of pioneering female scientists, doctors, activists, painters, dancers, astronauts, comedians, political leaders and many more from different walks of life.

TIMELESS
BIOGRAPHIES